THE
REINCARNATION
LIBRARY

The
SCALES
OF
KARMA

Owen Rutter

AEON PUBLISHING COMPANY

Mamaroneck

New York

First Published 1940

©2000 by Aeon Publishing Company, LLC
This edition has been designed and typeset
exclusively for The Reincarnation Library.
All rights reserved.

ISBN: 1-893766-09-8
Library of Congress Control Number:
99-76090

PRINTED AND BOUND IN THE UNITED STATES
OF AMERICA.

FOR

My Daughter

Contents

The SCALES OF KARMA

ONE

The Law of Karma

To-day, as perhaps never before in history, men and women are looking for a faith. Many are clinging to beliefs and dogma in which they were brought up, because they can find nothing to replace them. Others have fallen back upon passive agnosticism. The churches of to-day are half empty: not because those who have left them are irreligious, or have no need of spiritual comfort, but rather because the Church can no longer

THE SCALES OF KARMA

satisfy minds which are unwilling to accept teaching without question. The growth of education, and the conditions under which they live, have impelled them to question and, receiving no answer to which either logic or commonsense can respond, they turn away in despair.

They are told that God is omnipotent and benevolent. How then, they ask, can he permit man's inhumanity to man? Why does he allow the enemies of religion to triumph and to oppress? How can he tolerate the apparent injustice they see on every side? They can no longer accept the answer that all this is the will of God, and that the ways of God are inscrutable. Perplexed and bewildered, they turn aside.

I have been one of them. The Power which I believed must direct life upon this planet seemed to be without plan. Like most people who live in an ordered community, I wanted to feel that I was living in an ordered universe. Yet I could see no order, only chaos. With thousands of others, I was appalled by the human suffering throughout the world, by the unequal distribution of happiness, by what seemed to me the aimlessness of human life.

"Certainly while we still try to cling to the old theories of permanent personality, and of a single incarnation only for each individual," wrote Lafcadio Hearn in *Gleanings in Buddha Fields,* "we can find no moral meaning in the universe as it exists. Modern knowledge can discover no justice in the cosmic process; the very most that it can offer us by way of argument is that the unknowable forces are not forces of pure malevolence, 'neither moral nor immoral,' to quote Huxley, 'but simply unmoral.' Evolutional science cannot be made to accord with the notion of indissoluble personality . . . and if we are each and all mere perishable forms of being—doomed to pass away like plants and trees—what consolation can we find in the assurance that we are suffering for the benefit of the future? How can it concern us whether humanity becomes more or less happy in another myriad ages, if there remains nothing for us but to live and die in comparative misery? Or, to repeat the irony of Huxley, 'What compensation does the

Eohiphus get for his sorrows in the fact that some millions of years afterwards, one of his descendants will win the Derby?' "

As Professor W. MacNeile Dixon points out in *The Human Situation*, since the Renaissance there has been no such upheaval of thought, no such revaluation of values, as in the century upon which we have entered. Within the span of a single lifetime all the old conceptions, the previous beliefs in science, in religion, in politics, have been transformed. And with what result? Specialists offer us new theories in every branch of human enquiry, "but for a conspectus, a unifying creed, the plain man knows not where to look, and is plunged into a sea of perplexity. He reads one book to find its conclusions flatly contradicted by the next he opens."

Professor Dixon shows that the achievements of science, "those notable victories of the mind," from which so much was hoped, have, ironically enough, made for dejection rather than rejoicing. We know more than ever was known: and are convinced that we know nothing of what we most wish to know, for science has failed to minister to the needs of the soul.

"God and the soul," declares Professor Dixon, "are set aside as outworn superstitions, and the denial of any future life rings the passing bell of Christianity. Even the believers in unlimited human progress, that child-like and charming nineteenth-century creed, are beginning to have their doubts. Christianity, or what remains of it, has suffered a sea-change, and is fast melting, if it has not wholly evaporated, into humanitarianism."

He does not believe that the decay of religious faith is due to the increase of our positive knowledge, or that it can be ascribed to any degeneration in human nature. Men's hearts are what they have always been, nor are they now more inclined to vice than to virtue. "During the past century the rising tide of knowledge carried away all the old landmarks, the guiding light by which Christian Europe had steered its course, and the ship of religion is now labouring in a heavy sea." He believes that this is because of religion's inability to meet the needs of the intellect, to answer the innumerable and pressing questions we daily ask ourselves. Christianity has failed to solve the intellectual and moral problems which beset those who live in the complexities of the modern world.

Many rational people must share this mental perplexity to-day, just as I once shared it myself. But there came a time, some seven years ago, when I began to study the doctrine of Karma and Reincarnation. Although the subject had always attracted me, it was long before I understood enough of its implications to be able to accept it without reservation. After I had done so, quandaries which bewildered me before were made clear. I found a logical answer to every problem of human behaviour, an explanation of every form of suffering which once had seemed unjust, of every reward which had seemed unmerited. I came to understand why I was here, what I was doing, where I was going. I gained courage and confidence from this new attitude to life.

Although I am by profession a writer, I have hitherto written little upon this subject. In a novel I published recently I tried to show how belief in

Karma and Reincarnation affected the life of a girl who faced life alone and earned her own living. Although this was a thread running through the book it was not the main theme, but it brought me a number of letters from readers who were strangers to me, asking to know more, and finally I came to the conclusion that a fuller explanation of the subject, as I understood it, might be of help to others.

I have never been a missionary. I have an abhorrence of those who dogmatize and tell others what is best for them. I would as soon rob a blind man as attempt to undermine another's belief in a religion or a set of principles which he sincerely holds. Both as a man and as a writer I have a passionate belief in personal liberty of action and thought, expression and belief. For that reason I am writing this book as a personal statement rather than as an essay on Karma. It may seem more egoistical, but to me it is more modest. I attempt to prove nothing, because I know how few things are capable of proof: I cannot even prove to a friend that I have a headache, however much my head happens to be aching. I do not pretend that my opinions are worth more than those of anyone who reads this book: for opinion rests between the known and the unknown, between ignorance and knowledge, whereas faith is conviction based upon experience.

I have, therefore, been content to put forward my personal convictions. I make no attempt to convince others, for I know that few people have ever been convinced by argument, but I feel that those who cannot accept my views will at least respect them, since I have set them down with all the sincerity at my command. Those who already believe in the same principles as I, may find that details of my belief vary from theirs in a manner which may give them cause for thought; and if there are some who are able to find in these pages consolation in trouble, and explanation in perplexity, I shall not have written in vain.

I do not of course pretend that, in expounding the Law of Karma, I am giving a new set of ethics to the world. The teaching is as old as earth, perhaps older, since to me it seems unlikely that this is the only planet on which life has undergone spiritual evolution. On the other hand the doctrine of Karma, like all other teachings, has become encrusted with dogma since it was first expounded by those who understood it, and I believe that I present it here in its true form, as the wisdom which is the foundation of all the great religions of the world.

In its essence Karma is the law of cause and effect. It is adjustment rather than punishment. That is to say, although a man cannot escape the consequences of his actions, he can suffer only when he himself has made suffering necessary, just as he can receive only those blessings which he himself has earned, either in his present or some previous life.

Thus Karma differs from the Greek conception of Nemesis, which is the statement of only one side of the case. Nemesis and the avenging furies were represented as pursuing man to punish him for actions committed in this life. It took no account of his actions in other lives, nor did it give him recompense for his good deeds. It was merely a kind of supernatural criminal code administered by judges away from earth. It was half the truth, but not the whole truth. For karmic justice implies that, while every man must, sooner or later, pay his debts, he is equally entitled to collect the debts owing to him, and to enjoy the rewards which he has rightly earned.

The Law of Karma is defined, succinctly and adequately, in two texts in the Bible, one in the Old Testament, the other in the New:

"They that plough iniquity and sow wickedness, reap the same." (*Job*, *iv*, 8),
and

"Be not deceived; God is not mocked: for whatsoever a man soweth, that shall he also reap." (*Galatians*, *vi*, 7).

Suffering is thus not the will of God, nor is it unjust, for man can receive only that to which he is entitled.

Those who can accept this teaching see in the perplexities of life the logic and justice which they have hitherto sought in vain. To others, those who cannot accept it, the doctrine is an uncomfortable one. A man who has his house burgled may not find it agreeable to think that he himself may have robbed in the past and is now due to make practical and adequate adjustment. He would prefer to see himself the victim of untoward circumstances and wallow in self-pity. But because the Law may be damaging to self-esteem, that does not necessarily lessen its equity. Justice is commonly unpalatable to the convicted.

Karma, however, does not preclude free will. Nor does it imply an inhibiting fatalism which prevents a man struggling against his lot. Everyone has complete liberty to think as he will, speak as he will, act as he will. Each thought, speech and action will set up corresponding reactions which, sooner or later, will result in his being given a situation to face. How he faces it will depend entirely upon himself and upon the experience he has gained in the past. He may face it with wisdom, with courage, or with forbearance. Then he will have benefited by the experience gained and have extended his conscience. Or he may act with folly, cowardice or brutality. Then he will have failed, and will have to face a similar situation elsewhere, until he has learned his lesson.

Mr Somerset Maugham's short story, *The Gate of Opportunity*, will serve as an illustration. Alban Torel, a District Officer in the Far East, was in charge of a small outstation. He received a message that there was a coolie riot on an estate in his district. The coolies had killed the manager and burned the buildings to the ground. Torel's clear duty was to go with his police to the assistance of those who remained on the estate. He did not do so, preferring to wait for reinforcements rather than risk the lives of the small garrison under his command.

Here Torel was free to act as he thought fit. He could have done his duty, earned the approval of his superiors, and profited by the experience. But instead of grappling with the situation, he refused to face it, with the result that he suffered obloquy and was dismissed the service. He would therefore be set another test of courage, in a later life, until he had made adjustment.

In this case, which might well have happened in real life, Torel acted wrongly, by almost any standard of human ethics. Nevertheless, it is a man's motive, not the fallible opinion of his fellows, which must ultimately count in the assessment of Karma. In this brilliant psychological study, Mr. Maugham makes it clear that Torel was, at heart, a coward. But had he genuinely believed, without thought of his personal safety, that there was nothing to be gained by risking the lives of his men and that the wisest course was to wait, then, whatever view the world might have taken, he would surely have received full credit for his intentions by those who judged him away from earth.

Some of the most difficult decisions with which a man can be confronted are not those between right and wrong, but between right and right. If we turn from fiction to history, the case of Admiral Byng is not dissimilar from that of Alban Torel. Byng, it will be remembered, was court-martialled and shot for avoiding battle with the

French off the island of Minorca, where the British garrison was besieged, although Pitt protested against the sentence. There is, however, nothing to show that his motive in declining battle was disgraceful. The Government of the day had emasculated the fighting services. Lord Anson had mismanaged the Admiralty. Byng had been sent to the Mediterranean with a squadron of ten ill-equipped ships. He had orders to embark a battalion at Gibraltar, but the Governor had refused to deplete the garrison. The French had landed on Minorca and were besieging the castle of St Philip. On his arrival off the island Byng fought an indecisive action with the French fleet, and broke off the engagement at night-fall. He came to the conclusion that even if he were able to defeat the French, he had no troops to raise the siege, whereas a French victory would imperil the safety of Gibraltar. He therefore decided to retire to Gibraltar and to await reinforcements, leaving Minorca to its fate.

Here matters of high policy were at stake, and Byng acted in what he believed to be the best interests of his country. The result was that although England lost Minorca she retained possession of Gibraltar and command of the Straits. Byng's decision was not a glorious one. It was one that neither Nelson nor Rodney would have been likely to have taken; but there is no reason to presume that it was dictated by cowardice or treason. Byng's case is one which naval historians will never cease to debate, but it seems likely that, although some past action had made it necessary for him to suffer execution, his allotted karma would be different from Alban Torel's.

Another illustration of man's freedom of choice, and of this grave necessity of choosing between right and right, may be taken from contemporary history. In 1918, after the Armistice, Charles, Emperor of Austria and King of Hungary, went to live in Switzerland, and when the Bolsheviks and Rumanians who had occupied Hungary had been expelled, Admiral Nicholas Horthy, having created a national army, was elected Regent.

On Easter Sunday, 1921, the King appeared

unexpectedly at the Royal Palace in Budapest and demanded that the government should be handed over to him. Horthy was placed in a terrible dilemma. He had his duty to his country and his duty to his King, whose fleet he had commanded. But he knew that if he yielded to the King, Yugoslavia and Czechoslovakia, determined to prevent a Hapsburg restoration, would march into Hungary. He was free to act as he thought best, but here was a choice of loyalties, and he was well aware that whichever course he chose he would incur blame. Being a man of great integrity, with a passionate devotion to his country, he declined to support the King. To this day the Hungarian Legitimists have not forgiven him; but he earned the thanks of his country, which a restoration would certainly have destroyed.

Had he sided with the King, he had the justification of his oath. And if personal ambition, rather than altruism, had influenced his refusal, he would have failed to be true to himself, even though he had saved Hungary. None but the power which weighs motive can finally determine whether he acted rightly or no, but there seems little doubt that his decision was dictated by the wisdom gathered from experience, for, as George Eliot said,

Our deeds still travel with us from afar,
And what we have been makes us what we are.

T W O

The Granary of Memory

One of man's present difficulties has been to explain to himself why he is on this earth, but if one believes in an ordered universe, it follows that there must be a Plan which directs affairs. We are left to discover for ourselves the object of our lives, and it seems unlikely that it is not to gratify individual ambition.

Man and woman can scarcely have been placed on earth so that some may achieve power over others, or that some may secure wealth and success, while others live in poverty and humiliation. Nor can they be here merely to attain personal happiness, for if that were so how woeful is their failure.

I have come to believe that we are here to profit by every experience, both good and bad, that earth can give, so that gradually we may develop character and perfect our wills. To do that in one life would be impossible. As Professor Francis Bowen, of Harvard University, has said, "Three score years and ten must surely be an inadequate preparation for eternity." Therefore it must be necessary for us to return to earth again and again until we have learned every lesson, reaping as we have sown and learning to sow wisely that we may reap well, until we can reap perfection. In order that we may do this, and in order that the Law of Karma may be worked out, Reincarnation forms part of the Plan. It entails that we come to earth many times, in different bodies and in varying environments, incurring debts great and small, paying them off as we gain experience, profiting by what we learn, and acquiring such merit as we may, until each individual account is balanced and every debt is paid. Karma is thus the way to the fruits of experience, perfected wisdom. All the great teachers of earth have exhorted their immediate followers to seek wisdom: "Happy is the man that findeth wisdom and that getteth understanding." Since there can be no justice without wisdom, wisdom must hold the scales in which men's actions are weighed; and only after countless incarnations, profiting by the experience taught by the Law of Karma, can man reach perfection.

"To every awakened soul the question comes: Why does evil exist?" wrote Pascal. "So long as the enigma remains unsolved, Suffering remains a threatening sphinx, opposing God and ready to devour mankind. The Key to the secret lies in Evolution, which can be accomplished only by means of the continual return of souls to earth. When once man learns that suffering is the necessary result of divine manifestation, that inequalities of condition are due to the different stages which beings have reached and the changeable action of their will; that the painful phase lasts only a moment in Eternity, and that we have it in our power to hasten its disappearance; that, though slaves of the past, we are masters of the future; that, finally, the same glorious goal awaits all beings—then despair will be at an end; hatred, envy, and rebellion will have fled away; and peace will reign over a humanity made wise by knowledge."

I believe that people tend to reincarnate in groups, so that they may work out the karma incurred between them in other lives. Payment must be, I am sure, to the individual. If Smith has stolen from Brown, it is to Brown, not to Jones or Robinson, that he must, sooner or later, make restitution.

This individual responsibility is an essential part of the Law and precludes the possibility of racial or national karma. If there were such a thing as racial karma, the individual would have to endure collective suffering which he himself had not made necessary, or share in collective

advantages to which he was not personally entitled. At first thought it might seem as though this
were what does in fact happen, but even in a national disaster or a time of prosperity no two individuals' experience is exactly the same, although
that of the majority may be similar. In an earthquake there will always be some who will escape;
in a boom some who fail to profit.

On the other hand, many who shared in a sowing on a large scale may share in the reaping, be
the harvest good or bad. Thus it seems likely that
people who are due for similar karma tend to
reincarnate at the same period and in the same
country, gathered together to form a nation, not
fortuitously but as part of the Plan. The Belgians
who suffered so grievously in the German invasion of 1914 may have been a warlike tribe
which, earlier in history, conquered and enslaved
the group who reincarnated in Germany. Those
who took part in the civil war in Spain may have
fought a similar conflict in another life; while a
nation like the Hungarians, who have had to suffer by the mutilation and severance of large areas

of their country under the Treaty of Trianon, may in the past have enslaved the forbears of those Rumanians, Czechs and Yugoslavs who gained dominion over them in 1919. So, too, with the nations which Germany has invaded during the present war.

In the same way the reincarnation of groups of individuals with similar training accounts for the successive blossoming of the fine arts which have accrued at various periods of the world's history: Egyptian, Greek, Roman, the Renaissance, and in England and France later.

The principle that human beings reincarnate in circumstances suitable to the working off of their individual karma applies in heredity. Both the laws of physical heredity and the Law of Karma challenge the statement in the American Declaration of Independence: "We hold these truths to be self-evident, that all men are created equal." If all men alive to-day were in their first incarnation, that would be true: presumably we all started our chain of existence with a clean sheet; but since then each has written a different story. And upon that record depend the circumstances in which he will begin his new life. All mankind is one family, but its members are of different ages. Therefore there is no equality of opportunity and no equality of responsibility. Although all are marching towards a common goal they cannot bear equal burdens, and would not be expected to if the Law of Karma were understood.

In the physical laws of heredity there is nothing inconsistent with Reincarnation. A child's parents provide him with his physical body. If he has earned the right to a healthy body, he would be born to parents capable of giving him a robust and vigorous constitution, just as a gardener selects suitable soil for a particular plant. It is therefore natural that a child should resemble his parents physically. If the child has abused his body in a previous life, or if he has caused physical suffering to others, then he will be provided with weakly parents, or those who will be likely to pass on to him the disease which is necessary for him to experience. For example, a child who was due to suffer from tuberculosis would be sent to tubercular parents. The extent which he suffered from the disease would depend, not upon the degree of his parents' illness, but upon the gravity of the lesson he had to learn. It might be, for instance, that he had been a mine-owner whose men had contracted phthisis as a result of the conditions under which he made them work: thus he would have made it necessary that he himself should suffer in a similar way. The seriousness and length of his illness might also depend on the manner in which he faced his trial: for when he had worked out the karma which made his adjustment to suffering necessary it would be removed, and patience and fortitude might speed that adjustment.

Heredity provides the overcoat, but not its wearer. I do not believe that parents transmit mental qualities to their children, but a child who had to go through an incarnation insane might be placed with parents who were mentally afflicted, while one due for a brilliant academic career might be sent to parents of high intelligence or those who could give him the necessary education: unless, indeed, his karma made it necessary for him to win success only after a struggle against adversity, when his parents might be dull and indigent. This explains the clever child of clever parents, usually attributed to the result of heredity, and also the man who attains prominence from humble origin.

At the same time, because a child is born in favourable circumstances that does not necessarily mean that he will take advantage of his opportunities: the choice of action and career is his own. This accounts for the failure of children whose parents are in a position to give them every chance of advancement in a career, and also for the difference in achievement and character of members of the same family: if heredity were an exact process each child of the same parents should be true to type; and the reason why they are not, lies in the difference of their past experience.

Every child has the parents and the environment which he has deserved: it is for him to use or to misuse his opportunities, to rise above or succumb to poverty and neglect. The environment is the result of the use and abuse of past environments, and a knowledge of the Law of Karma must eliminate any feeling of superiority and inferiority. Those set in high places are entitled to all their position can bring. That surely is the meaning of Jesus's words: "Render unto Caesar the things that are Caesar's." It is ridiculous for a master to look down upon his subordinate, since in their next incarnations their positions may be reversed; and, for the same reason, the subordinate need not feel inferior to his chief.

Atavism may be explained by the fact that a child might be the reincarnation of one of his own ancestors. Temperament, character and individuality have nothing to do with heredity, except that a child who had to develop a certain line of training and experience would be sent to those most likely to provide him with suitable environment. I suggest that this is the explanation of children following one or other of their parents in their careers. It is easy to think of many in the circle of one's own friends, or among those in public life.

Sir Austen and Mr Neville Chamberlain, due for further training in political life, were born the sons of the champion of Protection. The late Mr W. B. Maxwell, due for further experience as a writer, had Miss Braddon for his mother. Miss Pamela Frankau is the daughter of a literary father, who is himself, like Mr Maxwell, the son of a woman novelist. Children due for similar experiences may reincarnate in the same family, as, for example, the Brontë sisters, or the Sitwells.

Then there are families with a long tradition in the fighting services, or in the law. These are clear and simple cases of children being placed in a family, and consequently in surroundings, suitable for the development of such talents as they have acquired in previous lives.

On the other hand, it is easy to think of many eminent people who have not followed their parent's calling. Often a man may become famous in an art or a profession in which his father may have had no part, one indeed which his family may object to his entering. Such a one was Shelley, the son of a Tory squire who was horrified that his son should want to be a poet. Such, too, was Captain James Cook, the son of an agricultural labourer. In our own time the portrait-painter Philip de László is a good example. He was born of humble parents in Budapest, yet from early childhood had no other wish but to become an artist.

What, then, is the truth of such men as these? Surely that past mistakes entailed that they could resume their previous training only by extending every effort of their wills and striving against adversity. The uncongenial family surroundings, and the obstacles to be surmounted, would then have a definite meaning and intention. Shelley, Cook, de László, each in his own way, and in his own degree, succeeded in attaining his desire through the force of his own character, allied to the talent with which he had reincarnated. And what could have given rise to that urgent desire but the memory of training in past lives—training forgotten, but persisting in the urge which sent poet, explorer and painter on the road to fame.

Balzac was of the opinion that "Laden with the

result of their past, and in possession of the capacities they have developed in the course of their evolution . . . men are philosophers or mathematicians, artists or *savants*, from the very cradle." What other explanation can there be of genius, which displays a like compulsion, but with more dramatic and spectacular results, as when a young musician such as Mozart begins playing with phenomenal mastery while still a child?

"The virtues we acquire, which develop slowly within us," wrote Balzac, "are the invisible links which bind each one of our existences to the others: existences which the spirit alone remembers, for Matter has no memory for spiritual things. Thought alone holds the tradition of the bygone life. The endless legacy of the past to the present is the secret source of human genius."

To many who study the subject, the most puzzling thing about Reincarnation is why, if we have existed before, we do not remember our past lives. A very few do; others imagine they do. Most people, when visiting some place for the first time in their present lives, have experienced the feeling of having been there before. Usually it is difficult to avoid mixing memory with imagination, and imagination with wishful thinking. I have noticed that most who profess to remember their past lives were nearly always people important either in Egypt or Ancient Rome. There are cases which can definitely be checked, but they are the exception. The ordinary man and woman—I among them—have no concrete remembrance of their pasts. As the Preacher said, "There is no remembrance of former things, neither shall there be any remembrance of things that are to come with those that shall come after."

Emerson wrote:

"But the Genius which, according to the old belief, stands at the door by which we enter, and gives us the lethe to drink, that we may tell no tales, mixed the cup too strongly, and we cannot shake off the lethargy now at noon-day. Sleep lingers all our lifetime about our eyes, as night hovers all day in the boughs of the fir-tree."

This inability to remember deters many from believing in Reincarnation. They do not stop to consider how fallible the untrained memory is. How many of us can remember what we were doing this day ten years ago? Of the year after we were born? As Tennyson wrote,

For is not our first year forgot?
The haunts of memory echo not.

"How many long passages of any one life are now completely lost to memory," declared Eustace Miles, "though they may have contributed largely to build up the heart and the intellect which distinguish one man from another."

It is the most difficult thing to recall and transcribe accurately a conversation which one has had with someone an hour previously, unless one has taken notes at the time. I have noticed this again and again when travelling abroad with the object of writing a book. Important people dislike discussing affairs with a man who spends his time scribbling notes. It makes them wary and clogs the flow of their discourse to see every word they utter being taken down. It is, at the least, an uncouth way to conduct a conversation. When in definite quest of information I found it helpful to repeat a sentence over in my mind, but even though one can train one's memory thus, it is essential to write down the gist of the interview as soon as possible, otherwise inaccuracy is almost inevitable. Is it strange, then, that without training we cannot remember the details of what happened in a previous existence?

I do not think it necessary that we should. We are here to face life in the present, not to peer into the past. Human beings have so much vanity, and so much curiosity, about themselves that they long to know what they were. Many may feel that such knowledge might help them to understand their present difficulties. The probability is, however, that such recollection would bring them little but pain. The obscuring of memory is surely merciful. The remembrance of all the wrongs we have done and all the wrongs which have been done to us, throughout our chain of lives would be an intolerable burden. Most of us have enough to contend with in this life, without burdening ourselves with the recollection of the dangers, the fears and the hates of other lives

Sir Arthur Conan Doyle once said, "We may point out that such remembrance would enormously complicate our present life," and suggested that "such existence may well form a cycle which is all clear to us when we come to the end of it, when perhaps we may see a whole rosary of lives threaded upon one personality."

I am prepared to accept the fact that a precise memory of other lives is not necessary to our present development. The German philosopher Lessing denied that forgetfulness of previous lives was a reason against believing in Reincarnation. "Happy is it for me that I do forget," he wrote. "The recollection of my former condition would permit me to make only bad use of the present. And that which I forget now, is that necessarily forgotten for ever?"

Fallibility of memory does not mean that memory is obliterated. I have no doubt that my actions, my thoughts, my spoken words, my hopes and fears are recorded upon the tablets of my memory and stored within its archives. Every writer who has set himself to draw upon his own recollections knows the extraordinary way in which the mists of forgetfulness roll back, revealing scenes and experiences long unremembered. As Mr Eustace Miles suggested in his book *Life After Life*, "The person with the balance at the bank may forget details of past accounts, knowing he has only £100 to his credit, and keeping the pass books and registers locked up, and perhaps having lost the key."

This shows that the memory of every event long past is but obscured, not wiped out; like a cigarette case dropped on a beach, it may be covered by the sand, but remains lying beneath the surface. In the same way, I believe, the memories of our other lives lie obscured from our recollection.

George Eliot put it thus in "The Spanish Gypsy":

Perhaps I lived before
In some strange world where first my soul was
shaped,

And all this passionate love, and joy, and pain,
That come, I know not whence, and sway my
*   deeds,*
Are old imperious memories, blind yet strong,
That this world stirs within me.

"Memory appears to be a palimpsest from which nothing is ever obliterated," declares Professor Dixon. "If we have forgotten most days and incidents of our present lives it is natural that memories of previous lives should fail us. Yet from infancy every forgotten day and hour had added to our experiences, to our growth and capacity. All that a child was and did, though unremembered, is still a part of him and is knit up into his present nature. Every day and hour had its value and made its contribution to the mind and soul. So it may be with former lives, each of them but a day in our past history."

That is to say, we are the sum of all our memories, although we may not have immediate possession of them. I say immediate possession because everyone has flashes of memory, even though he may not be conscious of them. Such flashes constantly affect personal relationships and social contacts. You may go to a cocktail party and meet a dozen people whom—to the best of your belief—you have not known before. Ten of them may leave you unstirred. You chat to them, and find them pleasantly agreeable or mildly uninteresting. They mean nothing to you. You would not care if you never saw them again. But to the eleventh you may take an instant liking. You find him—or her—what the French call *sympathique,* which means much more than our own word sympathetic. The response is immediate; you feel you have known one another for years. There may be no ostensible reason for this. The person you have met may be no more intelligent or charming or better-looking than the other ten to whom you have just been talking. But you get on together, and when you have left the party the remembrance of that one remains with you, fragrant and stimulating, an acquaintance to be pursued.

For this quick liking, to which you can ascribe no definite reason, what explanation is there but that you have found an old friend of a previous life and are but renewing a tie that has bound you close many times before? It is the explanation, too, of the unreasoning dislike you have taken to the twelfth person at the party. That dislike was immediate and, you had little doubt, was mutual. Yet here was a person whom others liked, whose manners were not outrageous, who said nothing at which you had any reason to take offence. The fact remained that you felt as repelled and uneasy in his company as you had felt at home in the presence of the eleventh. Here is the dim memory of an old aversion, the fumbling recognition of a former enemy, whom you had wronged, or who had wronged you.

The best definition I ever heard of memory was "The past, present." Thus both friendship and enmity are the present fruit of the past; and so with more intimate and more deeply emotional relationships. We often say of an acquaintance who is getting married, "What on earth can he see in her?" The bridegroom himself perhaps could not tell, nor the bride. To them it is as though the person for whom they have been looking all their lives has been found. And that, most likely, is the truth. For what can love be but the memory of an attachment in another life, just as hatred—if we are so unwise as to hate—the memory of an old injury unadjusted? This idea is simply and beautifully expressed in a Japanese poem translated by Lafcadio Hearn. In it the sense of the word *En* is what we should call affinity, and *Kwaho* good karma:

> *Love, it is often said, has nothing to do with*
> > *reason:*
> *The cause of ours must be some En in a previous*
> > *birth.*
> *Even the knot of the rope tying our boats to-*
> > *gether*
> *Knotted was long ago by some love in a former*
> > *birth.*
> *If the touching of sleeves be through En of a*
> > *former existence,*
> *Very much deeper must be the En that unites us*
> > *now!*
> *Kwaho this life must be—this dwelling with one*
> > *so tender—*

I am reaping now the reward of deeds in a former birth!

Since human beings are free to make or mar their happiness, and the happiness of others, friendships may be broken and love may appear to die. Friend may fail friend, and lover betray lover, but one of the happiest lessons of Reincarnation is that real friendship and true love must persist. In time reparation will be made, trust will be renewed, love bloom again more strongly than before, and in time the causes which led to hatred will be adjusted, so that friendship will result. Although by our own folly, or theirs, the friends of to-day may be the enemies of to-morrow, in the end our enemies must become our friends. That adjustment may—though it need not—take many incarnations to accomplish. The wise remember the saying "Agree with thine adversary while thou art in the way with him." Everyone has experienced the overcoming of that initial dislike—perhaps by some little act of kindness or better understanding—and the friendliness which results. Although it was a cynic who said that we should treat our friends as though they might one day become our enemies, there was wisdom in his corollary that we should treat our enemies as though they would one day become our friends.

As memory influences our personal relationships with the men and women we meet from day to day, so it accounts for our tastes or bent. I have shown how it must influence the choice of a career, but it can be traced in a thousand smaller events of our daily life. We have all had many forms of training in the past, and although we are following one particular line as our career in our present existences, that does not mean that the memory of other training is wholly obscured. So there is nothing remarkable in Mr Winston Churchill building walls in his spare time, or in Mr Neville Chamberlain going fishing whenever he has the opportunity.

Memory is the explanation, too, of a man turning from one form of activity to another wholly different: Joseph Conrad and Mr John Masefield leaving the sea to become writers, or Mr Somerset

Maugham and Dr A. J. Cronin turning from med-
icine to literature. They were free to choose their
careers. It may be that they followed one until in-
sistent memory called them to adopt the other, or,
since each has used in his books the knowledge
gained in his earlier profession, it may be that
they needed to gather this experience before em-
barking on what was to be their life's main work.

Others, perhaps, have missed the road they
might have taken, which accounts for their rest-
lessness and their impatience in their present oc-
cupations. Do we not all know the stockbroker
with a passion for the sea, the bank manager who
feels he could have commanded an army corps,
and quiet little Mr Jenkins, who lives in Strea-
tham and goes to his insurance office every day,
who has a passion for exploration? Those who
feel frustration now, and chafe at sitting on an
office stool, will have their chances again in
Karma's good time. Meanwhile, they solace themselves with hobbies and recreations—the would-
be sailor goes for cruises in the Mediterranean,
the bank manager plays with his son's toy sol-

diers, while Mr Jenkins reads every travel book he can lay hands on in the local Boots. Nowadays we hear much of the word "escapist." But this is not so much a desire to escape as of memory clamouring for fulfilment.

The most potent of these dimly stirring memories is fear, particularly those strange and unaccountable aversions which many of us have throughout our lives. Some can be explained by unhappy experiences in childhood, others only by terror we have felt in other lives. Psychologists have explained claustrophobia as a birth fear—the unpleasant experience every child must undergo in the act of being born. But if that were so, everyone would be frightened when he went in a lift. Is it not more logical to suppose that such fear is due to the memory of having been confined in a cell or dungeon in another life, an experience many of us have undergone? Or perhaps been overwhelmed by gas or water in a mine from which there was no escape? And the converse fear, agoraphobia—the fear of open spaces—may well be due to a man's memory of having been left alone on an open plain when the nomad tribe, or perhaps the army, to which he belonged moved on and left him to die. The inexplicable fear which some people have of feathers might be the memory of seeing the vultures gathering overhead as one lay dying on the plain—a fate that must have happened to many of us in the past.

All such irrational fears, that is to say fears for which there is no apparent cause such as loss of nerve through a motor accident or a fall from a horse, may be ascribed to this source, particularly when they persist beyond childhood. In my book *One Fair Daughter* I made the statement that children come into the world without fear, and that while fear takes root more readily in some minds than in others, it grows only from seeds which must first be planted. Now I would revise that generalization and say that the terrors from which young children so often suffer spring from seeds planted in their past lives. Parents and nurses are wiser nowadays than once they were, but while we may defend our children from fear by refraining from threatening to give them to sweeps, and by not telling them stories of ogres or letting them read Foxe's *Book of Martyrs* (that source of terror to many beside myself), we cannot control the fear that is their legacy from their own pasts.

Memory may also express itself in a flash of captured wisdom. This is the explanation of intuition, that strange guide whose presence no man can summon at will. It comes when we most need it, to give guidance or warning in an emergency, and we are wise to heed it, since its direction springs from experience learned in similar circumstances elsewhere. Why we act so, we cannot tell at the time: for it is not a matter of taking thought. Looking back afterwards, we can see that we acted rightly, but what made us do so we do not know; our action was simply the result of a flashed command, to be obeyed without question. Such was the case of the boy of fifteen who ran out into the street to stop a runaway horse. He had had no experience of horses in his present life, yet he seized the bridle fearlessly, brought the horse to a standstill and calmed it, as though he had been a stable boy. Afterwards, he could not tell why he had done what he did, but here, surely, was past experience flashing through, enabling him to deal efficiently with an unforeseen situation.

Inspiration is an even brighter flash than intuition. "You will ask me where I get my ideas," wrote Beethoven. "That I cannot tell you with certainty: they come unsummoned, directly, indirectly. I could seize them with my hands, while walking, in the silence of the night, at dawn, excited by moods which are translated by the poet into words, by me into tones that sound and storm and roar about me until I have set them down in notes."

What we call impulse I believe to be also akin to intuition: memory active, but not so vivid or so vital, and impulse may need to be controlled; while instinct is that form of memory which an animal brings back to earth from its group soul.

"The important thing . . . is to see that undoubtedly various orders of consciousness do exist, *actually embedded* within us," wrote Edward

Carpenter in *The Art of Creation*, "and that the words I and Thou do not merely cover our bodily forms and the outlines of our minds as we habitually represent them to ourselves, but cover also immense tracts of intelligence and activity lying behind these and only on occasions coming into consciousness. . . . To command these tracts in such a way as to be able to enter in and make use of them at will, and to bring them into permanent relation with the conscious ego, will I think be the method of advance, and the means by which all these questions of the perduration and reincarnation of the ego, and of its real relation with other egos, will at length be solved."

The most potent effects of memory are those exerted by the conscience, which is the granary of all experiences in other lives. It provides us with our individuality, which we bring back to earth with us life after life, each time enriched by the fresh lessons we have learned. Here all the wisdom we have gained in countless incarnations is enshrined, ready to warn against wrong-doing or to direct for good.

By listening to the dictates of his conscience a man is applying the results of his own experience. It follows that one who has been in incarnation many times will have what is called a more developed conscience than a "young soul" which has still many lessons to learn. In the dim past there was a time when each of us started on his first journey. In that first life he began to learn and began to make mistakes, thereby setting up karmic reactions which in time had to be adjusted. But because an action requires adjustment the lesson is not necessarily learned at once. Most of us must have robbed others many times before we learned, by repeated lessons, that stealing did not pay.

The conscience is thus limited by a man's own experience. If confronted by a fresh situation of which he has had no previous experience it cannot guide him with certainty, and he may then make fresh mistakes for which he will have to pay, adding to his knowledge of right and wrong. Of course in each earth life a child will be, or should be, taught the elementary lessons of right and wrong by its parents. But in the children of one family, all of whom have received the same training, the difference in individual memory can be seen, some members being amenable and others intractable, just as brothers and sisters differ in performance and achievement.

Once the lesson has been learned, the memory of it is established for future guidance. It is a wise saying that a man should never do what he knows to be wrong: that is, wrong for him, not necessarily for another. If he is in doubt, his conscience will tell him, so long as he is honest with himself and has ears to hear its warning tap.

THREE

Karma Precludes Chance

Karma, while it postulates free will, precludes a belief in luck or chance. The foundation of Karma is law, and a single instance of chance would nullify the Law and imply the fortuity of human affairs.

To those who come fresh to the conception of Karma this demands considerable mental adjustment. Most people are accustomed to regard luck, good and ill, as pervading their lives. Disappointed in their search for the meaning of life, and finding the creeds of their fathers no longer possible to accept, they turn from the idea of the omnipotent deity to the other extreme, and believe that the universe is ruled by chance, which is equivalent to saying that it is not ruled at all.

It is a strange conception. No business concern could be managed by trusting to luck: there must be direction, and disciplined effort to a definite end; the greater the attention to detail, the greater the prospects of success. The efficient business man leaves nothing to chance: why, then, should the Director of the Universe? And yet this belief in luck, and man's power to propitiate the god of fortune, has persisted through the ages, wherever men lost, or no longer heeded, the wisdom which taught that man cannot have anything, either good or bad, but that which he has earned.

That is the important point to remember. Why should we believe that we can mock God by snatching something we have not deserved? Or why should we be so lacking in faith as to think that the power responsible for the spiritual evolution of life should mete out suffering and what we call misfortune indiscriminately to the just and the unjust?

And yet to-day, in all the so-called civilized countries of Europe and America, a blind belief in luck sways humanity. Men and women envy those who to them seem favoured. They are the lucky ones. Those for whom nothing seems to go right are called unlucky. The lucky person is usually the other man, the unlucky ones themselves. Failure, or unexpected disaster, they ascribe to bad luck, without stopping to ask themselves whether that failure may not be due to their own lack of effort, or that disaster to something they may have done in the past, a lesson given them for their profit. Instead of examining their motives, they seek to attract good fortune or to ward off ill. The result is that the vendors of lucky charms do a thriving business, and so credulous is mankind that when the possessor of such a trinket enjoys a piece of prosperity he ascribes it, not to reward fairly earned by his own merit, but to the unexplained power of a lucky bean or a ring made from the hair of an elephant's tail. As Solomon put it in *The Book of Wisdom* (*xiii*, 18), "For health he calleth upon that which is weak: for life prayeth to that which is dead: for aid humbly beseecheth that which hath least means to help: and for a good journey he asketh of that which cannot set a foot forward."

It is at once a despairing and an arrogant philosophy. Despairing, because it leaves a man bereft of confidence in his own resources; arrogant, because it declines to recognize that he is responsible for his own suffering. So far from believing himself master of his fate and captain of his soul he is content to take his hand from the tiller of his will and to let himself drift.

I have come to believe that every instance of so-called good luck or misfortune is evidence of karma being worked out. The man who is lucky at cards has earned the right to be; the man who is unlucky in love is due to suffer because he has made others suffer in the past. So far as I can see, there can be no other satisfying explanation. We all know the man we believe to be wicked "in great power, and spreading himself like a green bay tree," as the Psalmist has it. We have so little faith, and so little understanding, that we question the justice of the divinity which can allow such a man to be in power and flourish, forgetting that it may be part of his karma to be exalted for a space, and given power to use for good or ill, so that if he indeed be wicked he will learn from his inevitable fall, as the next verse of Psalm 37 indicates: "Yet he passed away and lo, he was not: yea I sought him, but he could not be found."

Nor is there any need to take so extreme a case. In the circle of our own acquaintance, Jones, whom we know to be neither so efficient nor so hardworking as ourselves, goes ahead in his profession; we remain plodding behind. No one, with the possible exception of Jones himself, regards his advancement as being due to anything but luck, rather than to merit won in this or another life.

Or take Brown and Smith: Brown is lucky; he sells rubber short and the price falls next day; he switches round and becomes bullish: the price goes up. Smith, studying the markets far more carefully and acting on the considered information of the best broker in London, is invariably caught short when he should have been long, and long when he should have been short. He goes to Monte Carlo and comes back with £1000, while Smith, who stood beside him at the tables following a system, loses at every coup. At Newmarket Brown will back five winners out of seven, picking them off the card without studying the form, while Smith, who has worked out his own handicaps and spent hours with Ruff's *Guide* the night before, has an unpleasant account from Ladbroke's on Saturday morning.

And so through every phase of life. Luck seems to take precedence of efficiency. But every pound that Brown wins, another loses, and is due to lose it, just as Brown is due to win. That is to say, Brown wins because it is his karma to win. This may seem to amount to the same thing as luck. The effect is certainly the same, but the cause is entirely different. If Brown won by luck, it would mean that he made a profit irrespective of whether he had earned it or not. That, by the Law of Karma, is impossible. Brown has earned his right to win, just as Smith has made it necessary that he should lose.

It is interesting to speculate what would happen if Brown and Smith joined forces and gambled together. Would the syndicate win or lose? It would depend entirely on whether Brown's or Smith's karma were predominant. Here it might be that Smith had by that time earned the right to begin winning, or it might be Brown's karma to associate with Smith and thereby begin to lose what he had won. It seems a trivial matter, but those who look for worldly success will attain it best by associating in business undertakings with people whose karma appears to be good.

Myself I am one of the Smiths of this world. If I attempt to make money by gambling I invariably lose anything I may gain. Some years ago I made several hundred pounds by speculating in rubber on the produce market. Being greedy, I went on, lost it when the slump came, and more besides. I tried to get it back by gambling in cotton; did so, tried to make more, and failed. Eventually it seemed clear to me that I was being taught a lesson: that if I wanted to make money I must make it by my own efforts and not by gambling. I accepted the lesson and have not operated on the produce market since. I enjoy a flutter when I go to a day's race meeting, and, being an eternal optimist, I am always hopeful that I may succeed in making my bookie at least pay for the day's expenses, but so far the only monetary profit I have ever had out of racing was from a short story I wrote about a certain Mr Puddwater whose operations on the turf were no more successful than my own. But now I can at least leave the paddock at Newbury without any feeling of resentment against my bad luck. I have come to understand that it is not my karma to make money so easily as some of my friends seem to, and although I enjoy a day's racing and take more interest in a race if I have a modest bet, I accept the almost inevitable result with more equanimity than of old.

The Law of Karma stipulates, then, that there is no such thing as a game of chance, no such thing as a lucky day or lucky number. A dozen charms on a young woman's bracelet will bring her nothing she is unentitled to, nor is a talisman likely to ward off disaster or death. Those who have come to accept outrageous superstition as a substitute for religion may find this a preposterous doctrine: they must continue to spend their money on lucky beans, to wear white heather in their buttonholes, to avoid walking under ladders or looking at the new moon through glass. Those who can accept it, will, I think, find life and its meaning both saner and simpler, with less cause for heartburning at reverses and less reason for envy of those who appear to be in happier circumstances than themselves.

The belief in luck and the belief in fortune-telling run together. Here I find myself upon difficult ground. In recent years the belief that certain people can foretell the future has recurred to an extraordinary degree all over the civilized world. It is but another symptom of mankind's present discontent, and many are found to take advantage of it. Never before have the advertisements of psychometrists, palmists, astrologers, numerologists, crystal-gazers and all the rest of the great band of wizards who "peep and mutter" been so prominently and so blatantly displayed.

Astrology has, in particular, aroused the interest not only of the empty-headed but of serious people, many of whom have come to believe in it so firmly that they are prepared to direct both their business lives and their private actions by its predictions. I myself have been attracted to it and, failing to back winners either by studying form or by the less scientific method of shutting my eyes and putting a pin on my racing card, have gone so far as to cast horoscopes in the hope of finding the winner of the Grand National. I am fair-minded enough not to dismiss astrology as a fake because I have been unsuccessful. If it were as exact a science as its adherents claim it to be, it would be necessary to work out not only the horoscope of the horse, but those of his owner, his trainer and his jockey, and only if all indicated favourable aspects for the period during which the race was run could one expect to predict the result with any exactitude. Even if one applies the Law of Karma, difficulties arise in explaining why one horse should win and another lose, when there are so many people involved in its success or failure, and, obviously, it is impossible to know all the circumstances.

But taking astrology and the various other methods of foretelling the future in their widest sense, one is faced with the fact that certain predictions do come true. Many will be able to recall some predictions within their own experience or those of their acquaintances. I will mention one told me by a friend. A few years ago she was much exercised in her mind as to which of two men she should marry. Her sister recommended her to consult a fortune-teller. Rather unwillingly, she did so. The lady lived in Maida Vale. She was covered with beads and her room was hung with Japanese lanterns. She worked with cards. She told my friend that she would marry a dark man whose initials were K. H.—the K being a nickname.

"That's impossible," said Lavinia, "I finished with him twelve months ago."

She could identify the person mentioned, but as he was neither of the two with whom she was immediately concerned she left Maida Vale the poorer by half a guinea and so indignant that she scarcely stopped to think that it was curious that the fortune-teller should have got K. H. at all. Three years later she married him.

What is the explanation of such a prediction? Lavinia was free to make her own decision. She might have chosen either of the first two young men, but by free will she finally refused both; and by free will she eventually chose K. H. How, then, could the fortune-teller have known what she would decide three years before she made her decision? Some might say that the fortune-teller's words influenced her, consciously or unconsciously; but one had but to know Lavinia to be sure that such an explanation is unlikely. Or could the fortune-teller see the old relationship between those two, whose karma was that Lavinia must at least be given the opportunity to marry him? As against this, she had already had the opportunity more than once and had refused him, and so we cannot tell.

It must be admitted that human nature is such that one accurate prediction is remembered when a dozen inaccurate ones are forgotten. Nevertheless, a prediction whose accuracy can be checked and tested demands attention. Of course, if a score of diviners predict, let us say, the trend of international politics, the assumption is that at least one of their predictions may be right, just as one may expect at least one of a score of racing tipsters to give the winner of the Derby, and one hears much of his success and little of his colleagues' lamentable failures. But if divining were reliable every prediction of this nature should give the same result.

In August, 1939, a large number of astrologers did in fact reach the same conclusion—in predicting that war would not take place. We were told that the nations were to disarm, and that there was to be peace for ten years, with a unanimity which was as remarkable as it was encouraging to an anxious world. Then war came. The diviners explained their failure by insisting that although the stars point the way they cannot coerce, and that decisions must rest with man himself. But if, as the Law of Karma teaches, the Higher Powers do not take the initiative out of man's hands, how then can an astrologer or any other kind of diviner presume to foretell the future? How can he predict what has not begun, either in the politics of Europe or in the private life of an individual?

As I have said, every action a man does, sets in motion a sequence of results which spring from that primal cause. That he must face those reactions is inevitable; how he faces them is left to him. But until he has faced them neither he nor anyone else can tell what he is going to do.

Let us suppose that Mr William Mudge, in his present incarnation a Thames boatman, spent a previous life as a pirate in the Caribbean and forced the passengers in a captured ship to walk the plank. Let us also suppose that one of these passengers is now back in incarnation as a wealthy stockbroker, Mr James Fish. It so happens that Mr Fish hires a punt at Henley one afternoon. He is not an expert punter, and finding his pole stuck into the mud he clings on to it instead of letting go. The result is that the punt continues on its course downstream, leaving Mr Fish on the pole, which quickly subsides and deposits him into the river. There is a strong stream running towards the weir, and since Mr Fish cannot swim his predicament is not an enviable one, as he is the first to realize.

The only person within sight on the towpath at the moment is William Mudge. He is fifty years of age and somewhat corpulent, but when he sees Mr Fish wallowing in the water, obviously unable to swim, he realizes, without enthusiasm, that there are four courses open to him. He can continue his walk along the towpath, pretending not to have noticed Mr Fish's predicament, thereby saving himself from becoming implicated in an affair which he believes to be none of his business. Or he may stand on the towpath and shout advice to Mr Fish. Or, again, he may run off to procure a boat—by which time Mr Fish will probably either have gone down for the last time or disappeared over the weir. Lastly, he may whip off his coat to dive in and do his best to rescue Mr Fish, thereby adjusting his debt, perhaps at the cost of his own life.

Now I contend that while a person who had what are called clairvoyant powers might be able to predict the karmic situation with which Mr William Mudge would be faced, he could not tell what he would in fact do. There are many clairvoyants and palmists who would not claim to foretell more than that, but might advise upon a course of action in the predicted circumstances. Personally, I am not convinced that many can do as much, although I admit that those with certain powers, due perhaps to the dim memory of past training as seers, may be able to; but that they can foretell the future, that is, predict what William Mudge decides to do when he sees Mr Fish in the water, I cannot believe. For the same reason I would suggest, as an explanation of Lavinia's case, that the fortune-teller, being able to see the old tie between the two young people, based her prediction upon probability rather than knowledge.

As to astrology, if it were an exact science, no peculiar powers would be required, since anyone can learn to cast a horoscope which, if read according to the rules, should give the same results as a hundred others cast for the same person. But if one hundred people had cast Mr William Mudge's horoscope, would they have all predicted that extremely important incident in his career?

To me the chief argument against astrology is that none of the Great Masters ever used it. So far as we know, neither Krishna, nor Jesus, nor Gautama Buddha, ever mentioned it. Had it been possible to use it for the benefit of mankind, I cannot help feeling that they would have done so. Nor did any of the seers or prophets in the Old Testament make use of it. On the contrary, there are a number of prohibitions against divining of all kinds. The Pentateuch contains four explicit commands given by God to Moses:

"Thou shalt not suffer a witch to live." (*Exodus, xxii*, 18).

"Regard not them that have familiar spirits, neither seek after wizards, to be defiled by them." (*Leviticus, xix*, 31).

"The soul that turneth after such as have familiar spirits, and after wizards, to go a whoring after them, I will set my face against that soul and will cut him off from among his people." (*Leviticus, xx*, 6).

"There shall not be found among you any one that maketh his son or his daughter to pass through the fire, or that useth divination, or an observer of times, or an enchanter, or a witch, or a charmer, or a consulter with familiar spirits, or a wizard, or a necromancer. For all that do these things are an abomination unto the Lord." (*Deuteronomy, xviii*, 10).

Through the mouth of Isaiah, Babylon received this warning:

"Thou art wearied in the multitude of thy counsels. Let now the astrologers, the stargazers, the monthly prognosticators, stand up, and save thee from these things that shall come upon thee. Behold they shall be as stubble; the fire shall burn them; they shall not deliver themselves from the power of the flame." (*Isaiah, xlvii,* 13).

And again,

"When they shall say unto you, Seek unto them that have familiar spirits, and unto wizards that peep, and that mutter: should not a people seek unto their God?" (*Isaiah, viii,* 19).

It must be remembered that fortune-telling is quite different from prophecy. In the old days there were seers, or prophets as they came to be called later, who had been trained to communicate with the subtler planes and, by establishing direct contact with those away from earth—a process altogether different from mediumistic control—were enabled to obtain information which they could remember when they returned to their bodies. Such were Isaiah, Ezekiel, Samuel. That there may be people on earth to-day who have a vague memory of such training I am prepared to admit. They are the clairvoyants or clairaudients of to-day, but it seems likely that for every one who has such memory there are a score who merely profess to have.

The old training was abused, and later forgotten, yet throughout the centuries man's desire to learn the future has persisted. It seems extremely unlikely that the priestesses of the Delphic Oracle had any true power. They were the mouthpiece of a shrewd and well-organized intelligence system which was careful to safeguard its pronouncements by wording them ambiguously. The historic case was that of Croesus, who was told that if he crossed the river Halys he would overthrow the might of a great empire. He crossed it, only to find that his own empire was to be overthrown. Later the Romans tried divination by observing the flight of birds and the entrails of animals: a custom that persists to this day in Borneo, where the hill people, before going on a headhunting raid, consult the livers of pigs to ascertain whether the foray is likely to be successful or not. And to-day people in Europe and America still try

to consult the oracle by plying planchette and
ouija boards in their attempts to discover the way
in which karma will work out.

While I contend that no one can foretell what
has not begun, I am prepared to admit that one
with the necessary training may be able to foretell
death, so long as that death is not caused by self-
destruction. Thus, had Mr William Mudge flung
himself into the Thames in the hope of ending his
earthly troubles instead of with the object of res-
cuing Mr Fish, that action could not have been
foretold, since it would have been the result of his
own free will, uncontrolled by Karma. But had he
jumped in to rescue Mr Fish and been drowned in
the attempt, that action might have been possible
to predict, for, according to my belief, the time of
his death had been ordained since the day he entered his latest incarnation.

In this I hold that man has no choice. Against
each human being who comes to earth a mark is
set for the span of life. He may shorten that span,
but he cannot prolong it. "His days are determined," as Job declared, "the number of his

months are with thee, thou hast appointed his
bounds that he cannot pass."

A little thought will show that this is consistent
with the ordered Plan. If a man were able to prolong his life as he would, the working of the Law
would be defeated, since it must be part of his
karma to die upon a certain day, although in what
manner is not necessarily appointed. This explains why people are shepherded away from danger because their mark has not been reached.
Everyone knows of such cases. A good example is
that of an American whom I met in a railway car-
riage the day after the sinking of the *Athenia*. He
had come over in the ship with his wife and children, and had intended to take them back in her.
A few days before she was due to sail—before the
declaration of war—he had cancelled the passages. He could not tell why he had done so, for
he was anxious to get home. He had just "had a
kind of feeling" that he must.

On the other hand, no amount of playing for
safety will avail once the earthly span is complete,
as one may see by the case of the two little boys,

evacuated from the danger zone to Oxford. An aeroplane of the Royal Air Force slipped a practice bomb which went through the roof of the house where the boys were sleeping—in the same bed. One was killed, the other only injured: an example of the saying "The one shall be taken and the other left," and showing that in spite of the parents' care to safeguard the welfare of their child they could not keep him once the time had come for him to leave earth.

For myself, I shall always remember the night of an air raid in London during 1918. I was home on leave from Salonica, and dining at Princes with my cousin, Violet Gordon. We were just going on to Murray's when the raid began. Neither of us could see any reason why we should miss our dancing. We went outside into darkened Piccadilly—not so dark as it was to be in the next war—and the commissionaire found us a taxi. As he took his tip he said to me with a grin,

"That's right sir, you go on and enjoy yourself. They'll send for yer when they want yer!"

That, I firmly believe, was the exact truth. Nevertheless, although our span of life is determined we are not precluded from taking reasonable precautions for our safety, for we do not know the day or hour of our death, and it may be that if we expose ourselves foolhardily to danger we may reap karma in the shape of a broken leg.

If a man decides to go before he is sent for, however, and commits suicide, I believe that he will but have to suffer for trying to evade his responsibilities. God is not mocked: and he must return again to earth in another incarnation to make up the exact time he has cut short, and to undergo the experience that he had not the patience to endure. That time may be ten years or twenty. It may be a week; it may be that had he endured another hour he would have been free of his earth body. But back he must come to fulfil the Law, and this seems to me the only logical explanation of what we call the premature deaths of children and young people, which I used to think so meaningless and so unfair. But here, as always, the Law works with scrupulous justice, and children destined for an early death would be

sent to parents who, for some reason, had made it
necessary that they should suffer by such a loss.

Suicide, therefore, is both cowardly and foolish, and euthanasia, about which there is now
much discussion, in the long run avails the sufferer nothing, for if he leaves the world by the
hand of another at his own request, this must
rank as suicide. If his life is ended by the merciful
consideration of another, without his knowledge,
the case is different. Such "compassionate killing" is against the law and is likely to remain so,
but the courts treat such cases mercifully, although the accused person still has to go through
the ordeal and mockery of being sentenced to
death, when both judge and jury know there will
be a reprieve.

Here, one may suppose, Karma would strike
a balance. A mother, who, unable to bear the
sight of her idiot son's suffering, killed him in his
sleep, would have to make adjustment for breaking the law of the land, but so long as her motive
were truly compassionate, and without any tinge
of self-interest—such as wanting to rid herself

of the encumbrance and shame of a defective child—full credit would be given for her merciful intention.

Here, as always, the motive is all-important, and will invariably be taken into account. This is so even in man-made laws, for under the common law of England, the *mens rea*—the guilty intent— is the essence of a felony, and a man cannot be convicted of an offence unless he is proved to have committed it wilfully, or so long as there is a reasonable doubt that he knew what the consequences of his action were likely to be. Judge and jury may not be able to tell with exactitude the true motive of the human heart, but it can be weighed unerringly in the Scales of Karma. The results of an action may not be what the doer intended them to be: harm may arise from an attempt to do good, and good may come from an attempt to do evil, but no matter what the judgment of men may be, Karma will mete out ultimate justice.

The case of General Dyer is worth quoting as an example. In 1919 India was in a state of unrest.

The Muslims of the Punjab had joined the Hindus in agitating for political reform. Amritsar was the centre of revolt. Houses were burnt, several Europeans were killed, an English schoolmistress was murdered by the mob. General Dyer, who was in command, issued a proclamation prohibiting public meetings and threatening that they would be dispersed by rifle fire without warning. Nevertheless, that afternoon a crowd of several thousands assembled in the Jallianwalabagh, a large public garden, surrounded by high walls. General Dyer went to the garden with a small force of native troops. The meeting was being addressed by an agitator. General Dyer ordered his men to open fire without warning. Firing continued for ten minutes. There was no exit save by the way the troops had entered, although the General is said to have believed there was another gate. Over one hundred natives were killed, many more wounded.

This is not the place to discuss the rights and wrongs of the case, which is still an unhappy memory in India. After long inquiry General Dyer was removed from his post, and died shortly afterwards. But the revolt was ended, so that good came from immediate harm. There is no reason to doubt that General Dyer believed that he was doing his duty. So long as that was his motive, and so long as he was convinced that—as he declared—the mob was about to attack him, he would receive full credit for his intentions.

Because God is not to be mocked, and because karma, duly earned, is not to be escaped, a man should not submit to being submerged by a sea of troubles. This is where the doctrine of Karma differs from those of fatalism and predestination. There is wisdom in accepting an accomplished fact with resignation and equanimity, but until it is accomplished one may struggle against it with all one's might. If a man falls in front of a steamroller, he is not expected to lie down and let it go over him. No man knows his karma, and it may not be his to be run over. Therefore he is entitled to leap out of the way, or even put out all his strength to push the steamroller back, since this may be the particular effort he is required to make. It is the very act of struggling against adversity which develops will and character. The harder that struggle be, the more will the struggler gain, and so perhaps become entitled to have the karma removed.

Two small traders, Miller and White, may each be threatened with bankruptcy. Miller, refusing to be defeated, puts out all his energy, reorganizes his business, and by hard work and integrity staves off disaster. White, who had equal opportunities to do the same, lets his business slide to ruin, accepts what he calls the inevitable and takes the easy way out by going bankrupt and paying his creditors twopence in the pound. Miller has gained the right to his release from adversity, while White must face a similar situation again until he has learned his lesson. That lesson, the adjustment, may come soon or it may come late, in his present life, or after many lives.

One needs no knowledge of the Law of Karma to see cause and effect operating at every turn of human life. We are being taught by our own carelessness, lack of efficiency, and stupidity, all the time. If I am careless enough not to look where I am walking I may tread on a banana skin and bump my head: that will teach me to be more alert. If I have not sufficient foresight to wear an overcoat when there is an East wind blowing I probably get a raging cold in the head: that teaches me foresight. If I leave my umbrella in a taxi I have all the trouble of trying to recover it from Scotland Yard: that teaches me—or should—not to be absent-minded. The proverb that a burnt child fears the fire is but the expression of Karma working out in quick terms.

Faced with difficulties we must be, since we have made them necessary, but I do not believe that anyone is given a greater burden than his full strength can bear. If any lesson were too hard to be learned, there would be no point in it. It would be as futile as setting small boys in the Lower Fourth problems of the Mental Calculus, or asking them to construe Herodotus before they had learnt the Greek alphabet. It must surely be consoling to believe that every lesson we are being set is given us to test our wisdom, our tolerance, our loyalty, our honesty, our courage or our endurance. If we fail, as fail we must at times, we do so only because we allow ourselves to fall below our own standards, below the level we have reached, or have the ability to reach if we put out all our power.

In trying to put out that power, we are given help. The saying "As thy day is, so shall thy strength be" is true. Everyone familiar with those words must recall how he has been given strength to do something that once would have seemed impossible. The converse, "As thy strength is, so shall thy day be," must be equally true, since no one is called upon for more than past experience qualifies him. Moreover, what may appear to be misfortune may prove ultimately to be spiritual gain, and those in trouble and affliction will do well to bear these words in mind:

"Take comfort, for perchance the storm that shaketh thee shall be but the breeze to waft thee on thy way."

FOUR

The Teaching
in the Old Testament

More than half the inhabitants of the globe believe in Karma and Reincarnation and there is evidence to show that it is the oldest faith on earth.

"As this hypothesis is rational in itself, so it has gained the suffrage of all philosophers of all ages, of any note, that have held the soul of men incorporeal and immortal," declared Dr Henry More. "I shall add, for the better countenance of the business, some few instances herein as a pledge of the truth of my general conclusion. Let us cast our eye, therefore, into what corner of the world we will, that has been famous for wisdom and literature, and the wisest of those nations you shall find the asserters of this opinion.

"In Egypt, that ancient universe of all hidden sciences, that this opinion was in vogue amongst the wisest men there, the fragments of Trismegist do sufficiently witness: of which opinion, not only the Gymnosophists, and other wise men of Egypt, were, but also the Brahmans of India, and the Magi of Babylon and Persia. To these you may add the abstruse philosophy of the Jews, which they call the Cabbala, of which the soul's pre-existence makes a considerable part, as all the learned Jews do confess."

Herodotus mentions that the Egyptians were the first people to propound the theory of rebirth, and *The Book of the Dead*, or, more properly, *The Book of Coming Forth into Life*, which scholarship ascribes to a date even earlier than Manes, the first historical King of Egypt (c. 4777 B.C.), makes it clear that a belief in Reincarnation was the basis of the ancient Egyptian's faith. *The Book of the Dead* is the description of the journey of Ani the Scribe after death when he comes before the gods for the assessment of karma.

"Though my body be buried, yet let me rise up," prays Ani. "And may I come forth and overthrow my foes on earth."

And again:

"Homage to thee, O Governor of those who are in Amenti, who makest mortals to be born again."

There is also a passage in which Ani says, "Before Isis was, and when Horus was not yet, I had waxed strong and flourished," which shows his belief in his pre-existence.

The Egyptians are popularly supposed to have believed in a number of gods, many of whom had the forms of animals. But the following text shows their belief in a supreme deity: "God is one and alone, and none other existeth with him." It is likely, therefore, that the lesser gods were perfected beings, or masters, away from earth, from whom help might be sought, and that their animal form symbolized a particular attribute: thus, the ox would represent patience; the hawk, will; the serpent, wisdom; the lion, strength.

After death, the dead man appeared before these masters, when his deeds were weighed in the Scales of Tahuti. If he could recite the negative confession, and say in truth, "There is not in all the world a sinful one, a weeping one, a sorrowful one, through any act of mine," it was said of him, "Thy foot shall not be fettered in heaven, thou shalt not be turned back upon the earth."

In Egyptian symbology the god Tahuti, or Toth, personified wisdom, and therefore held the scales which weighed in their unerring balance the heart of man against the feather, which was the symbol of memory, or truth. If the balance were level the spirit had no need to go forth to suffer birth and death again, but if that perfected experience were still lacking, it had to tread the path of Reincarnation and Karma until the scales were balanced.

Of Horus, known as the Hawk God, it was said, "He bestoweth wickedness upon him that worketh wickedness, and right and truth on him that followeth after right and truth," while the following Pyramid text also refers to Karma: "If, having been of no account, thou hast become great, and if, having been poor, thou hast become rich, when thou art governor of the city be not hardhearted on account of thy advancement, because thou hast become the guardian of the provisions of God."

According to the Jewish Cabbala, belief in Reincarnation was held by Moses, whom Dr More describes as "the greatest philosopher certainly that ever was in the world," and the Talmud relates the legend that Abel's soul passed into the body of Seth, and then into that of Moses.

The Old Testament abounds in references to Karma, both in abstract teaching and in concrete and dramatic examples of the working of the Law. The metaphors of sowing and reaping, readily appreciated by the Hebrew mind, constantly recur, the harvest representing the result, or karmic reactions, caused by the sower of deeds. Here it may be noted that the ancient Egyptians symbolized garnered experience as "the ears of long-standing corn."

"He that soweth iniquity shall reap vanity," declared Solomon (*Proverbs, xxii*, 8), and "The sluggard will not plow by reason of the cold; therefore shall he beg in harvest, and have nothing." (*xx*. 4). "Sow to yourselves in righteousness," exhorted Hosea (*x*. 12), "reap in mercy; break up your fallow ground: for it is time to seek the Lord, till he come and rain righteousness upon you. Ye have ploughed wickedness, ye have reaped iniquity; ye have eaten the fruit of lies." Hosea's strange saying, "They have sown the wind, and they shall reap the whirlwind" (*viii*, 7), may be a warning to those who attempt to use forces which they cannot control.

Samuel, too, recognized the Law when he said, "The Lord rewarded me according to my righteousness: according to the cleanness of my hands hath he recompensed me." (*II. xxii*, 21). Then there is this comfortable promise of Psalm 126, "They that sow in tears shall reap in joy. He that goeth forth and weepeth, bearing precious seed, shall doubtless come again with rejoicing, bringing his sheaves (experience) with him."

Similar, too, is the promise that God shall render to every man according to his works (*Proverbs, xxiv.* 12), and that "The recompence of a man's hands shall be rendered unto him." (*Proverbs, xii.* 14).

The Law of cause and effect is epitomized in Proverbs, vi. 27–8: "Can a man take fire in his bosom, and his clothes not be burned? Can one go upon hot coals, and his feet be not burned?" And the following passages in the same book apply explicitly to the working of the Law:

"Whoso stoppeth his ears at the cry of the poor, he also shall cry himself, but shall not be heard" (*xxi.* 13) and "There is that scattereth, and yet increaseth; and there is that witholdeth more than is meet, but it tendeth to poverty. The liberal soul shall be made fat: and he that watereth shall be watered also himself." (*xi.* 24–5). "Rob not the poor, because he is poor: neither oppress the afflicted in the gate: For the Lord will plead their cause, and spoil the soul of those that spoiled them." (*xxii*. 22–3).

The following curious passage in Proverbs suggests that Solomon is referring to Reincarnation; "When he prepared the heavens I was there, when he established the clouds above, when he appointed the foundations of the earth, then I was by him, as one brought up with him, and I was daily his delight, rejoicing always before him, rejoicing in the habitable parts of the earth, and my delights were in the sons of men."

"It is visible," wrote Sir Thomas Browne, commenting on this text, "that Solomon speaks here of a time soon after the creation of the world, of a time when the earth was inhabited by a pure, innocent race. Can this be said after the Fall, when the earth was cursed? It is only a profound ignorance of the ancient, primitive tradition of preexistence that can make men mistake the true sense of this sublime text."

Another indication of Solomon's belief in Reincarnation may be found in his apocryphal saying "Being good, I came into a body undefiled." (*The Wisdom of Solomon, viii*, 20). The same book shows how the Egyptians had to work out their karma collectively in being plagued by the very creatures with which they had sinned: "For the foolish devices of their wickedness, wherewith being deceived they worshipped serpents void of reason, and vile beasts, thou didst send a multitude of unreasonable beasts upon them for vengeance; that they might know that wherewithal a man sinneth, by the same shall he also be punished." (*xi*. 15–6).

In Psalm 37, David recognized the eventual working out of Karma for the just and the unjust: "The wicked plotteth against the just, and gnasheth upon him with his teeth. The Lord shall laugh at him: for he seeth that his day is coming. The wicked have drawn out the sword, and have bent their bow, to cast down the poor and needy, and to slay such as be of upright conversation. Their sword shall enter into their own heart, and their bows shall be broken."

And again, in Psalm 7: "He made a pit, and digged it, and is fallen into the ditch which he made. His mischief shall return upon his own head, and his violent dealing shall come down upon his own path."

The same teaching is to be found in Proverbs, xi. 17–18: "The merciful man doeth good to his own soul: but he that is cruel troubleth his own flesh. The wicked worketh a deceitful work: but to him that soweth righteousness shall be a sure reward."

In Ecclesiastes there are many references to Karma: "He that diggeth a pit shall fall into it; and whoso breaketh an hedge, a serpent shall bite him" (*x*, 8); and again "Cast thy bread upon the waters: for thou shalt find it after many days." (*xi*, 1). Here bread might be taken to refer symbolically to individual experience and the waters to the flow of spiritual evolution, the meaning being that if one places one's wisdom at the disposal of evolution one will have one's reward in time. A similar implication is to be found in verse 6 of the same chapter: "In the morning sow thy seed, and in the evening withold not thine hand: for thou knowest not whether shall prosper, either this or that, or whether they both shall be alike good."

Elsewhere (*v.* 8) the Preacher refers to the Law of Karma in his explanation of the apparent injustice of human affairs: "If thou seest the oppression of the poor, and violent perverting of judgment and justice in a province, marvel not at the matter: for he that is higher than the highest regardeth; and there be higher than they;" and in *xii,* 14 he adds, "For God shall bring every work into judgment, with every secret thing, whether it be good, or whether it be evil."

The story of Job is perhaps the most dramatic example in Biblical history of individual karma being worked out. Here was a man "perfect and upright," who feared God and eschewed evil. He was a man of substance and great possessions, and he used them well. By the standard of human justice the disasters which came upon him appear inexplicable. There is no suggestion that, in the incarnation in which he then was, he deserved chastisement. But it may well be that he had erred greatly in past lives and still had to learn to sustain patience in adverse circumstances. It may be, too, that, wishing to work out his karma quickly, he himself asked that he might be tested in the way he was. If this explanation can be accepted, what followed becomes intelligible: Job brought upon himself terrible sufferings in order to learn quickly the lessons that might have been spread over many lives. The first lessons he accepted with fortitude: the loss of possessions, the capture of the oxen and asses by the Sabeans, the burning of the sheep, the taking of the camels by the Chaldeans, and the slaughter of his herdsmen. He bore the sudden death of his children when his eldest son's house was destroyed by a gale of wind. Professing his belief in Reincarnation, and accepting the justice of the Law, he said, "Naked came I out of my mother's womb, and naked shall I return thither: the Lord gave, and the Lord hath taken away; blessed be the name of the Lord."

Even when he was afflicted with boils "from the sole of his foot unto his crown" his resolution did not fail him for a time. In reply to his wife's words, "Dost thou still retain thine integrity? Curse God and die," he said, "Shall we receive good at the hand of God, and shall we not receive evil?" Not until after seven days' suffering in silence did he open his lips and curse his day. Nor was he comforted when his friend Eliphaz the Temanite said, "Remember, I pray thee, who ever perished, being innocent? or where were the righteous cut off? Even as I have seen, they that plow iniquity, and sow wickedness, reap the same. . . . Behold, happy is the man whom God correcteth: therefore despise not thou the chastening of the Almighty."

The orations of Eliphaz, and those of Bildad and Zophar which followed, were indeed little calculated to assuage the agony of an afflicted man. By that time Job's wisdom and patience had been obscured. "The arrows of the Almighty are within me," he cried, recognizing the working of Karma but, in his distress, refusing to accept it, and begged for death. His friends continued to utter their sententious platitudes until, exasperated as many another has been since by a plethora of speeches, he demanded, "How long will ye vex my soul, and break me in pieces with words?" and continued to protest his integrity and to bemoan his karma.

Elihu, "fetching his knowledge from afar"—that is, by contact with subtler planes—rebuked Job for his presumption, showed him the justice of the Law and warned him that judgment had taken hold on him, since he had chosen iniquity rather than affliction. Then, in some of the finest passages of the Bible, God taught Job humility, until, his lesson learned and his pride humbled, he repented, so that "his end was blessed more than his beginning." Thus he came to understand that it is unwise to ask to be allowed to work out karma precipitately, since "sufficient unto the day is the evil thereof."

Job was punished for sins committed in a previous existence, but the story of Nebuchadnezzar, King of the Chaldeans, shows how karma may be speeded up for the adjustment of offences com-

mitted in the same life. In order that Nebuchadnezzar might learn humility, and know in his
pride that "the most High ruleth in the Kingdom
of Heaven, and giveth it to whom he will," he was
deposed from his throne and, as related in the
Book of Daniel, "driven from the sons of men;
and his heart was made like the wild beasts, and
his dwelling was like the wild asses: they fed him
with grass like oxen, and his body was wet with
the dew of heaven, till his hairs were grown like
eagles' feathers, and his nails like birds' claws."

Nevertheless, as in the dream which Daniel interpreted the stump of the tree roots was allowed
to stand after the tree had been hewn down, so,
when Nebuchadnezzar had learned his lesson
and his understanding had returned to him, he
praised God and was established in his kingdom
once more.

Of such karma being worked out, the Bible has
many examples; but perhaps none more poignant
than that of Moses, who earned the karma of seeing but not entering the Promised Land.

One of the most misunderstood passages of the

Old Testament is the commandment "Thou shalt not make unto thee any graven image . . . for I the Lord thy God am a jealous God, visiting the iniquity of the fathers upon the children unto the third and fourth generation of them that hate me." (*Exodus, xx.* 4–5). Although this commandment is repeated every Sunday in every church in the Kingdom, how many of the congregation stop to think what gross injustice it implies if taken literally? Any humane person would protest if he saw a child being thrashed for an offence committed by its father. How, then, can one accept the fact that God, who should be the fountain of justice, punishes sinners' descendants who have no share in their parents' or ancestors' blame?

Moreover, if read literally the commandment would be in direct opposition to the Law of Moses: "The fathers shall not be put to death for the children, neither shall the children be put to death for the fathers: every man shall be put to death for his own sin" (*Deuteronomy, xxiv,* 16), an injunction which was expressly regarded by Amaziah, who slew the murderers of his father

Joash, but not their children, as related in the second book of Chronicles.

If, however, the commandment is explained in terms of Reincarnation it becomes clear, for the person who had committed an offence in the past would be back in incarnation in the third or fourth generation and would then have to face the consequences of acts done in his previous life.

Nowhere in the Old Testament is the teaching of the Law more beautifully set forth than in the fifty-eighth chapter of Isaiah, where the prophet transmits the teaching obtained by direct contact from his master in an exhortation to his people to abandon dogma and the outward profession of belief for the realities of loving-kindness: the lesson which is the foundation of the Law and the basis of the teaching of Krishna, Gautama Buddha, and Jesus:

"Behold, in the day of your fast ye find pleasure, and exact all your labours. Behold, ye fast for strife and debate, and to smite with the fist of wickedness: ye shall not fast as ye do this day, to make your voice to be heard on high. Is it such a fast that I have chosen? a day for a man to afflict his soul? is it to bow down his head as a bulrush, and to spread sackcloth and ashes under him? wilt thou call this a fast, and an acceptable day to the Lord? Is not this the fast that I have chosen? to loose the bands of wickedness, to undo the heavy burdens, and to let the oppressed go free, and that ye break every yoke? Is it not to deal thy bread to the hungry, and that thou bring the poor that are cast out to thy house? when thou seest the naked, that thou cover him; and that thou hide not thyself from thine own flesh? Then shall thy light break forth as the morning, and thine health shall spring forth speedily: and thy righteousness shall go before thee; the glory of the Lord shall be thy reward. Then shalt thou call, and the Lord shall answer; thou shalt cry, and he shall say, Here I am. If thou take away from the midst of thee the yoke, the putting forth of the finger, and speaking vanity; And if thou draw out thy soul to the hungry, and satisfy the afflicted soul; then shall thy light rise in obscurity, and thy darkness be as the noonday: And the Lord shall guide thee continually, and satisfy thy soul in drought, and make fat thy bones: and thou shalt be like a watered garden, and like a spring of water, whose waters fail not."

FIVE

The Teaching of Krishna

According to tradition, Krishna was born about 1500 B.C.—fifty years before the date ascribed to the five books of Moses. His parents were related to one of the petty kings of India. The story of his birth in a cowshed, and of the slaughter of the children owing to the King's fear of a prophecy that a child should be born who should sway all India, closely resembles the story of Jesus in the New Testament. To save the child's life he was hidden away and brought up by a shepherd, and, after he had fulfilled the prophecy by spreading his teaching throughout India, he met his death by being pinned by an arrow to a tree.

Revelation came to him as a young man, and his teaching is embodied in the *Bhagavad-gita*, the Sanskrit poem which occurs as an episode in the sixth book of the Hindu epic *Mahabharata*, one of the five jewels of Devanagiri literature. Its doctrine remains to this day the essential part of the Brahmin religion, and the closeness of its teaching to that of Jesus has, like the facts of Krishna's life, given rise to controversy between the Pundits and the Christian Church as to whether the author borrowed from Christian sources, or the writers of the Gospels from the *Bhagavad-gita*. Scholarship now tends to accept the fact that the *Bhagavad-gita* was incorporated in the *Mahabharata* at a date considerably later than the original poem, but there is evidence to show that it was written before the Christian era.

The scene of the poem is the level country between the Jumna and the Sarsuti rivers—now

Kurnul and Jheend. A great battle is impending, and Krishna takes on mortal form as the charioteer of Prince Arjuna, who is leading his army against his enemies, among them his own kinsmen. The poem is in the form of a dialogue between Krishna and the Prince, in the war-chariot on the field of battle.

Arjuna, to whom the identity of his charioteer has been revealed, gazes upon the opposing host and, just as a general might feel to-day, is reluctant to give the order which must lead inevitably to loss of life. In anguish he cries to Krishna:

> *Shall I deal death on these*
> *Even though they seek to slay us? Not one blow,*
> *O Madhusudan! will I strike to gain*
> *The rule of all Three Worlds; then, how much less*
> *To seize an earthly kingdom! Killing these*
> *Must breed but anguish, Krishna! If they be*
> *Guilty, we shall grow guilty by their deaths;*
> *Their sins will light on us, if we shall slay*
> *Those sons of Dhritirashtra, and our kin.**

*This, and the quotations which follow, are taken from *The Song Celestial*, Sir Edwin Arnold's translation of the *Bhagavad-gita*.

Having made his plea, Arjuna sinks back upon
his chariot seat and lets his bow and arrow fall.
But Krishna rallies him to his duty as a warrior
prince and calls upon him to fight. Arjuna again
protests, whereupon Krishna explains to him
more gently that the spirit cannot die, and that it
is the spirit, not the earth body, which matters:

> *Thou grievest where no grief should be! thou*
>   *speak'st*
> *Words lacking wisdom! for the wise in heart*
> *Mourn not for those that live, nor those that die.*
> *Nor I, nor thou, nor any one of these,*
> *Ever was not, nor ever will not be,*
> *For ever and for ever afterwards.*
> *All, that doth live, lives always! To man's frame*
> *As there come infancy and youth and age,*
> *So come there raisings-up and layings-down*
> *Of other and of other life-abodes,*
> *Which the wise know, and fear not. This that*
>   *irks—*
> *Thy sense-life, thrilling to the elements—*
> *Bringing thee heat and cold, sorrows and joys*
> *'Tis brief and mutable! Bear with it, Prince!*
> *As the wise bear. The soul which is not moved,*

The soul that with a strong and constant calm
Takes sorrow and takes joy indifferently,
Lives in the life undying! That which is
Can never cease to be; that which is not
Will not exist. To see this truth of both
Is theirs who part essence from accident,
Substance from shadow. Indestructible,
Learn thou! the life is, spreading life through all;
It cannot anywhere, by any means,
Be anywise diminished, stayed, or changed.
But for these fleeting frames which it informs
With spirit deathless, endless, infinite,
They perish. Let them perish, Prince! and fight!
He who shall say, "Lo! I have slain a man!"
He who shall think, "Lo! I am slain!" those both
Know naught! Life cannot slay, Life is not slain!
Never the spirit was born; the spirit shall cease to
be never;
 Never was time it was not; End and Beginning
 are dreams!
Birthless and deathless and changeless
 remaineth the spirit for ever;
 Death hath not touched it at all, dead though
 the house of it seems!

Who knoweth it exhaustless, self-sustained.
Immortal, indestructible—shall such
Say, "I have killed a man, or caused to kill?"
   Nay, but as when one layeth
      His worn-out robes away,
   And, taking new ones, sayeth,
      "These will I wear to-day!"
   So putteth by the spirit
      Lightly its garb of flesh,
   And passeth to inherit
      A residence afresh.

Here is a perfect exposition of the doctrine of
Reincarnation, with its discrimination between
the things of the spirit, which are permanent, and
the things of earth, which are impermanent.
Krishna assures Arjuna that no weapon can touch
the spirit, flame cannot burn it, or waters over-
whelm it:

   Impenetrable,
Unentered, unassailed, unharmed, untouched,
Immortal, all-arriving, stable, sure,
Invisible, ineffable, by word
And thought uncompassed, ever all itself,

Thus is the Soul declared! How will thou, then—
Knowing it so—grieve when thou shouldst not
    grieve?
How, if thou hearest that the man new-dead
Is, like the man new-born, still living man—
One same, existent Spirit—wilt thou weep?
The end of birth is death; the end of death
Is birth: this is ordained! And mournest thou,
Chief of the stalwart arm! for what befalls
Which could not otherwise befall? The birth
Of living things comes unperceived; the death
Comes unperceived; between them, beings
    perceive:
What is there sorrowful herein, dear Prince?

Once again Krishna calls upon Arjuna to do his
part and tremble not, since,

Nought better can betide a martial soul
Than lawful war,

and warns him that if, knowing his duty and his
task he lets them go by, that shall be his sin, and
bring infamy upon his name.

He goes on to pour scorn on the dogma of the Brahmins, just as Jesus did upon the Pharisees, urging Arjuna to free himself from "that sad righteousness which calculates" and to shake off "those tangled oracles that ignorantly guide," so that he may find full reward of doing right in right:

> *Let right deeds be*
> *Thy motive, not the fruit which comes from them.*
> *And live in action! Labour! Make thine acts*
> *Thy piety, casting all self aside,*

until, "troubled no longer by the priestly lore," he attains Yog and Peace—which is union with the divine. He tells Arjuna:

> *That man alone is wise*
> *Who keeps the mastery of himself! If one*
> *Ponders on objects of the sense, there springs*
> *Attraction; from attraction grows desire,*
> *Desire flames to fierce passion, passion breeds*
> *Recklessness; then the memory—all betrayed—*
> *Lets noble purpose go, and saps the mind,*

Till purpose, mind, and man are all undone.
But, if one deals with objects of the sense
Not loving and not hating, making them
Serve his free soul, which rests serenely lord,
Lo! such a man comes to tranquillity;
And out of that tranquillity shall rise
The end and healing of his earthly pains,
Since the will governed sets the soul at peace.

The condemnation of dogma and asceticism is an essential part of Krishna's teaching. He shows that there are three ways of setting up karma—by soothfastness, which binds the soul to happiness and truth, by passion, which "binds to toilsome strain," and by wilful ignorance, which obscures the light of wisdom and binds the soul to sloth:

These three bind down
The changeless Spirit in the changeful flesh.

The gift lovingly given, when he who accepts it has nothing to give in return, is soothfastness; the gift given for a purpose is stained with passion; while the gift churlishly flung in disdain is the gift of ignorance, and does not bless.

Once passion and ignorance are overcome, soothfastness remains, causing the lamp of knowledge to shine through all the gateways of the body; and so, in the lives to come, the fruit of man's labours is threefold: desirable and undesirable, and a blend of both, but not fruit at all is there where no work was.

> *When a soul departeth, fixed*
> *In Soothfastness, it goeth to the place—*
> *Perfect and pure—of those that know all Truth.*
> *If it departeth in set habitude*
> *Of Impulse, it shall pass into the world*
> *Of spirits tied to works; and, if it dies*
> *In hardened Ignorance, that blinded soul*
> *Is born anew in some unlighted womb.*

Krishna taught that "right action" is that which, being enjoined, is wrought for duty, not for gain; "vain action" that done to satisfy desire; and "dark action" is that which is heedless of results upon others or upon the self.

> *Whoso performeth—diligent, content—*
> *The work allotted him, whate'er it be,*

Lays hold of perfectness! Hear how a man
Findeth perfection, being so content:
He findeth it through worship—wrought by
    work—
Of Him that is the Source of all which lives,
Of Him by Whom the universe was stretched.
Better thine own work is, though done with fault,
Then doing others' work, ev'n excellently.

He insists that only he whose purpose remains unswayed by his emotions, and only he who has the mastery of his will, to be won by meditation, can attain perfect wisdom.

Whereupon Arjuna asks, if meditation be nobler than action, why Krishna exhorts him to fight. Krishna then explains that there are two schools of wisdom, the two great roads of conduct—action, or works prescribed by reason, and inaction, or the road of spiritual meditation. Yet these two roads lead to the same end, since no man may escape responsibility by shunning action, and none shall reach perfection by mere renunciation. Man's nature compels him, however unwilling, into action:

But he who, with strong body serving mind,
Gives up his mortal powers to worthy work,
Not seeking again, Arjuna! such an one
Is honourable. Do thine allotted task!
Work is more excellent than idleness;
The body's life proceeds not, lacking work.

Krishna's insistence on action was an integral part of his teaching that each must play his part and do the work that comes to him, and that it is better that he should do it as best he can, even though he may fail, than tasks not his own, however good they may seem—just as we say that a cobbler should stick to his last.

At the same time he declares the danger of becoming earthbound to action, and teaches that man must be quit of fear and hope, and with equal calm accept whatever may befall, not over-glad in joy, or over-sad in sorrow.

> *Call*
> *That the true piety which most removes*
> *Earth-aches and ills, where one is moderate*
> *In eating and in resting, and in sport;*

Measured in wish and act; sleeping betimes,
Waking betimes for duty.

This is what Gautama Buddha was to call the Middle Way. Krishna taught that man, having passed through all experience, attains unity with Being:

His soul to the Supreme Soul, quitting sin,
Passes unhindered to the endless bliss
Of unity with Brahma. He so vowed,
So blended, sees the Life-Soul resident
In all things living, and all living things
In that Life-Soul contained.

This unity with Brahma is the equivalent of the Nirvana of Buddha, the Kingdom of Heaven of Jesus.

Arjuna protests that it were as easy to hold the wind as to hold a man's heart. Krishna agrees that man's heart is hard to restrain, but assures him that a man may learn to be master of himself "by wont of self-command." When Arjuna asks what will befall one who has faith but fails, Krishna compassionately answers that no heart which holds one right desire "treadeth the road of Loss."

> *He who should fail,*
> *Desiring righteousness, cometh at death*
> *Unto the Region of the Just; dwells there*
> *Measureless years, and being born anew,*
> *Beginneth life again in some fair home*
> *Amid the mild and happy. . . .*
> *So hath he back again what heights of heart*
> *He did achieve, and so he strives anew*
> *To perfectness, with better hope, dear Prince!*

Thus at last he may free himself from "the chain which holdeth men to good and evil issue." To such a one:

> *Grief and joy*
> *Sound as one word; to whose deep-seeing eyes*
> *The clod, the marble, and the gold are one;*
> *Whose equal heart holds the same gentleness*
> *For lovely and unlovely things, firm-set,*
> *Well-pleased in praise and dispraise; satisfied*
> *With honour or dishonour; unto friends*

And unto foes alike in tolerance;
Detached from undertakings—he is named
Surmounter of the Qualities!

Krishna then speaks of the banyan tree, whose branches shoot to heaven and sink to earth, even as the deeds of men, a beautiful description of Karma. He shows that man may reach perfection by the growth of new actions

Upspringing to that happier sky,—
Which they who reach shall have no day to die,

having attained that rest which is "life's utmost boon."

Having given Arjuna the outline of his philosophy, Krishna again calls upon him to destroy the enemies of his kingdom, telling him that he is but the instrument of Karma: he will but slay the slain. They must fall, as he must live, their conqueror.

If this day thou say'st,
Relying on thyself, "I will not fight!"
Vain will the purpose prove! thy qualities

Would spur thee to the war. What thou dost shun,
Misled by fair illusions, thou wouldst seek
Against thy will, when the task comes to thee
Waking the promptings in thy nature set.
There lives a Master in the hearts of men
Maketh their deeds, by subtle pulling-strings,
Dance to what tune He will. With all thy soul
Trust Him, and take Him for thy succour, Prince!

To which Arjuna replies:

Trouble and ignorance are gone! the Light
Hath come unto me, by Thy favour, Lord!
Now am I fixed! my doubt is fled away!
According to Thy word, so will I do!

Although much in the teaching of Krishna may
seem a counsel of perfection, nevertheless allowance is made for those who have still far to go
upon the road. But the keynote of the teaching
is, as in the teaching of Buddha and Jesus, that
a man should not become too deeply attached
to the things of earth. Krishna, like every other
Great Master, taught the qualities of compassion,

kindness, patience and unselfishness, tolerance, faithfulness, and freedom from anger, arrogance and greed: in a word, the virtues of self-control from which spiritual balance is attained: so much, in some degree, is within the power of every man and woman to learn.

> *Fearlessness, singleness of soul, the will*
> *Always to strive for wisdom; opened hand*
> *And governed appetites; and piety,*
> *And love of lonely study; humbleness,*
> *Uprightness, heed to injure nought which lives,*
> *Truthfulness, slowness unto wrath, a mind*
> *That lightly letteth go what others prize;*
> *And equanimity, and charity*
> *Which spieth no man's faults; and tenderness*
> *Towards all that suffer; a contented heart,*
> *Fluttered by no desires; a bearing mild,*
> *Modest, and grave, with manhood nobly mixed,*
> *With patience, fortitude, and purity;*
> *An unrevengeful spirit, never given*
> *To rate itself too high;—such be the signs,*
> *O Indian Prince! of him whose feet are set*
> *On that fair path which leads to heavenly birth!*

Here indeed is a teaching which can be applied to everyday modern life. Some will find it strangely close to the more familiar words of the Sermon on the Mount. In reality it is not remarkable that the teaching of Krishna and Jesus should be similar; nor is there any need for scholars and theologians to debate whether the lessons of the *Bhagavad-gita* were learned from the Gospels, or whether the Gospels borrowed from the *Bhagavad-gita,* for both taught the principles of wisdom, founded on truth; and these cannot vary, no matter in what country or in what century they are expounded.

SIX

The Teaching of Gautama

Perhaps no teaching of the Great Masters has
been so misunderstood in the West as that of
Gautama Buddha. Yet, in its wisdom, it was the
teaching of Krishna and Jesus. It was a teaching
of moderation and tolerance, of reason and common sense.

Cease to do evil,
Learn to do well,

The Teaching of Gautama

Cleanse your own hearts:
This is the teaching of the Buddha.

Buddha is the term applied to one who has attained enlightenment, and so might have been applied to Krishna or to Jesus; but Gautama did not become known to his followers by this title until a century after his death; and to-day is known as Buddha to thousands who are ignorant of his teaching.

Gautama was born in India on the borders of Nepal, to the north-east of the present province of Oudh. Some authorities place his birth as early as 620 B.C., others as late as 563 B.C., so that he was teaching at the time the Phocaeans were founding Marseilles, when Cyrus was ruling Persia, when Pythagoras was in Athens, and when Lao Tsze was in China.

Gautama was his family name. His personal name was Siddhartha—and his father, Suddhodana, was ruler of the Sakyas: in later legend represented as a great king, but in fact perhaps not more than a feudatory prince. Gautama was brought up in luxury, excelled in knightly accomplishments, and was married to a Sakya girl called Yasodhara, with whom he fell in love at their first meeting, memory stirring so that he knew they were not strangers; and long afterwards, when full enlightenment had come to him, the story goes that he was able to recall the time in a former life when he was a hunter's son and she a forest girl to whom he "gave a tame fawn and his heart's love beside."

His married life did not endure for long. He longed to know the reason of existence. Yearning for the truth, he found himself unable to accept the pretensions of the Brahmin priestcraft, and became restless in the luxury with which his father surrounded him. It is said that Suddhodana, fearing the prediction that his son would become a hermit, tried to keep from him all knowledge of human misery. In this he failed, and Gautama eventually left Yasodhara and his young son to adopt a homeless life of the wandering ascetic, so that he might strive ceaselessly to attain wisdom by personal experience and discover how he could liberate men from the bondage of mortality and rebirth.

He sojourned in one hermitage and another, following every known ascetic practice, outdoing others in penance, self-denial and in solitude. He went without clothes, and fasted in the woods, until, as legend had it, he could subsist upon a single grain of rice a day, and until his body became so wasted that, in the words of the Pali Canon, his belly clung to his backbone for lack of sustenance.

At length he came to understand that self-torture was not the road to enlightenment. Abandoning his life of solitude, he begged his way from village to village as a mendicant friar, and one day took his seat beneath a jambu-tree, resolving that he would not move until he had attained supreme enlightenment.

He is represented, like Jesus, as being tempted by Mara, the Evil One, and as he emerged unscathed from the ordeal, he was enabled to see, as Sir Edwin Arnold describes in *The Light of Asia,*

The line of all his lives in all the worlds;
Far back, and farther back, and farthest yet,
Five hundred lives and fifty.

Arnold likens him to a man who rests upon a mountain summit and looks back upon the path by which he has made the long ascent. Also he saw:

How new life reaps what the old life did sow;
How where its march breaks off its march begins;
Holding the gain and answering for the loss;
And how in each life good begets more good,
Evil fresh evil; Death but casting up
Debit or credit, whereupon th' account
In merits or demerits stamps itself
By sure arithmic—where no tittle drops—
Certain and just, on some new-springing life;
Wherein are packed and scored past thoughts
*   and deeds,*
Strivings and triumphs, memories and marks
Of lives foregone.

The Law of Karma and the doctrine of Re-incarnation, upon which Gautama's teaching is founded, was accepted by the Hindus of the time, just as it was accepted by the Jews in the time of Jesus. But whereas pre-Buddhist thought taught that the soul, like "an ethereal mannikin," as Dr Ananda Coomaraswamy puts it in *Buddha and the Gospel of Buddhism*, removed from one body to another, Gautama nowhere taught the transmigration of souls—that is, of the astral and mental bodies or what we call personality—but only the transmigration of spirit, which is character and individuality, the sum of experience gathered up to that point. He likened life to a flame: transmigration, new becoming, rebirth, is as though one candle were being lighted from another: the flame continues to endure, but the candle is different.

Mr Coomaraswamy suggests as another illustration the analogy of two billiard balls: if one ball is rolled towards another, the moving ball will stop dead, and the contacted ball will move on. The first ball in motion does not continue its course, it remains behind, it dies, but it is the momentum of that ball, its karma, and not any newly-created movement, which is reborn in the second ball.

"Buddhist reincarnation is the endless transmigration of such an impulse through an endless series of forms," says Mr Coomaraswamy. "Buddhist salvation is the coming to understand that the forms, the billiard balls, are compound structures subject to decay, and that nothing is transmitted but an impulse, a *vis a tergo*, dependent on the heaping up of the past. It is a man's character, and not himself, that goes on."

Like Krishna and Jesus, Gautama taught that men must progress towards spiritual evolution, and this disposes of the popular fallacy that he taught that the spirit might retrogress by reincarnating in the bodies of animals.

Gautama's teaching was not written down until four centuries after his death. Although writing was introduced into India during the eighth century before Christ, the mnemonic system was by that time so perfect that no need of the written word was felt. The sutra, or string, of aphorisms was the usual literary form of Gautama's day, and

almost all early Indian literature is composed in
verse. But in about 80 B.C., when the followers of
Gautama were beginning to fall away from his orthodox teaching, the Canon was compiled in the
Pali language, in Ceylon, that the true doctrine
might endure; nevertheless this Buddhist Bible,
like that of the Christians, consists of books composed at different periods, by different hands.

Gautama outlined his teaching in his first
sermon, which he preached in the deer park
at Isipatana, near Benares. The lesson he emphasized was moderation in all things: the Middle
Way between realism and nihilism, between
wordly pleasures and self-mortification which,
with Krishna, he held to be "painful, unworthy,
unprofitable." By avoiding these two extremes he
himself, he told his disciples, had been able to
gain understanding of the Middle Way which, in
the words of the Pali Canon, "giveth Vision,
which giveth knowledge, which causeth Calm, Insight, Enlightenment, and Nirvana."

The Middle Way may be defined as the steadily
increasing application of the abstract virtues,

unhampered by belligerent fanaticism or passive agnosticism. Gautama's doctrine (dharma) is defined in four axioms, or Noble Truths: That suffering exists; that suffering has a cause; that the cause can be eliminated; that there is a way—the Eightfold Path—by which this may be done.

He taught that the Eightfold Path consisted of eight stages of personal experience:

Right Faith: in the four axioms.

Right Purpose: for renunciation, non-resentment, harmlessness.

Right Speech: abstinence from lying, backbiting and gossip.

Right Conduct: abstinence from taking life, from taking what is not given, from wrongdoing in sexual passions.

Right Living: abstinence from wrong living.

Right Effort: the perfecting of the will to inhibit evil conditions which have not yet arisen, to reject evil conditions which have arisen, to cause the arising of conditions that have not yet arisen to establish and cause the increase and fulfilment of good conditions that have already arisen.

Right Mindedness: self-possession which can control the covetousness and dejection of earth.

Right Rapture, or Contemplation: this last step consists of four stages. The first is directed and sustained thought upon a definite objective. The second stage is reached by the sinking down of such directed thought until an inner calm is achieved, and the sublimation of the will. This leads to balance, until at last, rejecting pleasure and pain, the seeker after truth enters the fourth stage, free from either joy or sorrow, a state of perfect purity and equanimity.

This Eightfold Path, then, was the way leading to the extinction of suffering. And Gautama taught that suffering was birth, and decay, sickness, old age and death; likewise sorrow and despair. Contact with the undesired was suffering, and separation from the desired, also frustration and denial. The origin of suffering was craving for gratification or sensation, the will to be born again, also the desire to have done with rebirth. The extinction of suffering was the passionless emancipation from this craving by the elimination of desire—to be found only through the Eightfold Path, which is the Middle Way.

Gautama cautioned his disciples against excess of zeal, and once, instructing one who had been skilled in lute playing in his youth, he said:

"When the strings of your lute were too taut, were they fit to play upon?"

"No, Lord," was the reply.

"But when they were neither too taut nor too slack, but evenly strung, did your lute not give out music?"

"It did, Lord."

"Even so," said Gautama, "excess of zeal makes for self-exaltation, just as lack of zeal makes for sluggishness. Wherefore, persist in evenness of zeal, master your faculties, and make that your mark."

In Buddhist teaching, Karma is likened to the wheel of a wagon, the idea being that Karma follows thought and action, good or bad, as inevitably as the wheel which follows the ox that draws a cart.

When teaching the Law of Causation, Gautama explained that actions are determined by ignorance, and that consciousness is determined by actions. From consciousness is evolved mind and body—sense, contact and feeling, and by feeling arises craving—for shape, sound, scents, savours, tangible things and for ideas. Craving leads on to grasping, which leads to birth, "the seizing hold of the spheres of sense," and birth to age and death, sorrow and despair. From the cessation of ignorance comes the cessation of actions, and so on through the chain of causation until, by the cessation of becoming and of birth, comes the end of age and death, sorrow and despair. That is to say, all activities may be set at rest, and all roots of being severed, by the destruction of craving, which leads to passionlessness and Nirvana. Gautama told the brethren that this Law of Causation was difficult to understand, beyond the sphere of thought, to be penetrated by the wise alone; and that since the world of men clung to things of earth it was hard for them to grasp. But by failing to heed it they had become entangled like a ball of twine and so were unable to pass beyond the ceaseless round of rebirth.

He warned his disciples against mere lip-service, and against learning his words by heart without meditating upon their meaning. He likened him who did so to a man searching for water snakes: he might find a large one, and grasp it by the tail; the snake might turn back on him and bite him, causing a wound that would lead to suffering and death. Even so might those who wrongly grasped the doctrine come to suffering.

As to daily behaviour, Gautama's teaching was identical with that of Jesus, in that he counselled lack of resentment, meekness and forbearance. When one of his disciples complained that the others had mocked him, he was told that it was not seemly that one who himself had a sharp tongue should not endure the tongues of others; and on another occasion, speaking to one who had suffered abuse, he said:

"If anyone to thy face should abuse thee . . . if he were to strike thee with fist or hurl clods of earth at thee, or beat thee with a stick, or give thee a blow with a sword—yet must thou set aside all worldly desires, all worldly considerations, and thus must thou train thyself: 'My heart shall be unwavering. No evil work will I send forth. I will abide compassionate of others' welfare, and kindly heart without resentment.' "

He continued this lesson in the parable of the saw, and explained to his disciples that when a man spoke evil of them, they must suffuse him with thoughts accompanied by love, and so abide; and, making that their habit, they must suffuse the whole world with loving thoughts, "far-reaching, wide-spreading, boundless, free from hate, free from ill will."

"Moreover, brethren," he continued, "though robbers, who are highwaymen, should with a two-handed saw carve you in pieces limb by limb, yet if the mind of any one of you should be offended thereat, such an one is no follower of my gospel."

He called upon them to bear this parable for-ever in their minds. Is not this the teaching of the Sermon on the Mount?

Like Jesus, too, Gautama taught that hatred is never appeased by hatred, but only by kindness. He emphasized the need of showing goodwill to all men. These are his injunctions for "him who is wise to know what is good for him":

"He must be able and upright and truly straight: gentle of speech and mild, not having vain conceit of self.

"And he should be content, soon satisfied, with but few wants, of frugal appetites: with faculties of sense composed, discreet, not insolent, nor greedy after gifts.

"He should do no mean thing for which other men who are wise may censure him. . . .

"Let none deceive another, nor think scorn of him in any way whatever. Let him not in anger or ill-will desire another's ill fate.

"Even as a mother, as long as she doth live, watches over her child, her only child,—even so should one practice an all-embracing mind unto all beings.

"And let a man practice a boundless goodwill for all the world, above, below, around, in every way, goodwill unhampered, without ill-feeling or enmity. . . .

"Thus shall a man, by passing over wrongful view, by walking righteously, be gifted with insight and conquer greed for sense-desires. Of a truth such an one shall come no more to birth in any womb."

On another occasion he compared "treasure laid up on earth" to the treasure of good deeds. By charity, by righteousness, by self-restraint, and the taming of the self, woman or man may win treasure which robbers cannot steal. "Let the wise man do good deeds: that is the treasure that follows after me."

He taught his disciples to be thankful and grateful for all service, so that the slightest boon should not be given to them in vain; and although he performed no miracles or acts of healing, he impressed upon them the need of caring for the sick.

There is an incident related in the Pali Canon which recalls the story of the Good Samaritan. Upon a certain day Gautama and his disciple

Ananda came upon a monk who was suffering from dysentery and had been deserted by the brethren. He sent Ananda for water, tended and washed the sick man, and laid him upon the bed. Then he assembled the brethren and said, "You have no mother and no father to care for you. If you will not care for each other, who else will do so? Brethren, he who would wait upon me, let him wait upon the sick." So Jesus said, "Inasmuch as ye do it unto one of these little ones, ye do it unto me."

Gautama clearly drew a distinction between Karma and predestination. Karma does not absolve a man either from responsibility, or from the duty to make his effort; it is an active doctrine, not passive; but it does assert that "the order of nature is not interrupted by miracles": man must find deliverance from within, and Right Effort is an essential part of the Buddhist doctrine. In its essentials Buddhism is not a religion of abstention, as some have declared. The injunction "Cease to do evil" may imply abstention, but to "learn to do well," and "cleanse your own hearts" are exhortations to put forth all the strength of which a man is capable.

In this Buddha taught what others had taught before him. It would be a mistake to suppose that he evolved a new religious philosophy. Like every other Great Master, he did but recall to men's minds the wisdom which had been forgotten, and degraded by animism and superstitious ritual. And while Gautama did not explain how continuity of karma passed from one individual existence to another, and indeed took the survival of spirit—though not of soul—for granted, there was nothing inconsistent in his teaching with the Brahmanical doctrine that a subtler body, the vehicle of character, remains unimpaired by death and eventually reincarnates in a new physical body, carrying with it the experience and the corresponding karma collected in previous lives. When Gautama himself speaks—as reported in the Pali Canon—of his own intercourse with the gods and his visits to their heavens, he was no doubt describing his experiences when in touch with subtler planes away from earth, like the prophets in the Old Testament.

But just as Jesus reserved his most profound truths for "those who had ears to hear," so did Gautama, teaching the simpler lessons to the uninstructed. He likened himself to a farmer who devotes most care to his most productive fields— the disciples, or brethren—less attention to the less fertile fields—the Buddhist laity—and less still to the barren soil—those who did not accept the Law.

He showed no desire to confound the views and practices of other sects. He expressly stated that he was willing to teach any upright man of intelligence who came to him. But he had no desire to win pupils, or to make others fall from their religious vows, or give up their ways of life. Like Jesus, however, he had little patience with recluses and sectarians. They were blind and unseeing, he told his disciples. They knew neither the real nor the unreal, neither the truth nor the untruth; and quarrelled in ignorance. To illustrate his point, he told the story of the rajah who gathered together all the blind men in his capital and commanded that they be shown an elephant. Each was to be allowed to feel a certain part, one the head, another the ear, one the tusk, another the trunk.

"Have you studied the elephant?" asked the King at last.

"Yes, Your Majesty," answered the blind men.

"Then tell me your conclusions about it."

Thereupon he who had touched the head declared, "Your Majesty, the elephant resembles a pot." He who had felt the ear said the elephant was like a winnowing basket. Another who had touched the tusk said the elephant was a ploughshare, and the one who had felt the trunk said it was a plough. The body was a granary, the foot a pillar, the back a mortar, the tail a pestle. They began to argue and dispute, much to the King's delight.

Even so, said Gautama, were the sectarians who, knowing not the truth, each maintained it was thus and thus.

The time came when Buddhism itself fell from its pristine wisdom to narrow dogma, and no part of the Master's teaching has been more misinterpreted than the lesson of Nirvana, which is often represented as total effacement or obliteration.

"There still widely prevails in Europe and America the idea that Nirvana signifies, to Buddhist minds, neither more nor less than absolute nothingness,—complete annihilation," wrote Lafcadio Hearn in *Gleanings in Buddha Fields.* "This idea is erroneous. But it is erroneous only because it contains half of a truth. This half of a truth has no value or interest, or even intelligibility, unless joined with the other half. And of the other half no suspicion yet exists in the average Western mind.

"Nirvana, indeed, signifies an extinction. But if by this extinction of individual being we understand soul-death, our conception of Nirvana is wrong. Or if we take Nirvana to mean such reabsorption of the finite into the infinite as that predicted by Indian pantheism, again our idea is foreign to Buddhism.

"Nevertheless, if we declare that Nirvana means the extinction of individual sensation, emotion, thought,—the final disintegration of conscious personality,—the annihilation of everything that can be included under the term 'I,'—then we rightly express one side of the Buddhist teaching.

"The apparent contradiction of the foregoing statements is due only to our Occidental notion of Self. Self to us signifies feelings, ideas, memory, volition; and it can scarcely occur to any person not familiar with German idealism even to imagine that consciousness might not be Self. The Buddhist, on the contrary, declares all that we call Self to be false. He defines the Ego as a mere temporary aggregate of sensations, impulses, ideas, created by the physical and mental experiences of the race,—all related to the perishable body, and all doomed to dissolve with it."

Literally translated, Nirvana means the dying out of the unworthy, the dross consumed. As the process of reincarnation consists in the transference of the flame of spirit from one individual existence to another, so the dying out of the flame, no longer kindled by the fires of emotion, signified the peace of the individual who is no longer dominated by the will to live, and thus reached Nirvana and self-realization.

"Unconsciously dwelling behind the false consciousness of imperfect man," continued Lafcadio Hearn in the same essay, "beyond sensation, perception, thought,—wrapped in the envelope of what we call soul (which in truth is only a thickly woven veil of illusion), is the eternal and divine, the Absolute Reality: not a soul, not a personality, but the All-Self without selfishness,—the *Muga no Taiga*,—the Buddha enwombed in Karma. Within every phantom-self dwells this divine: yet the innumerable are but one. Within every creature incarnate sleeps the Infinite Intelligence unevolved, hidden, unfelt, unknown,—yet destined from all the eternities to waken at last, to rend away the ghostly web of sensuous mind, to break forever its chrysalis of flesh, and pass as to the supreme conquest of Space and time. . . .

"The striving for Nirvana is a struggle perpetual between false and true, light and darkness, the sensual and the supersensual; and the ultimate victory can be gained only by the total decomposition of the mental and the physical individuality. Not one conquest of self can suffice: millions of selves must be overcome. For the false Ego is a compound of countless ages,—possesses a vitality enduring beyond universes. At each breaking and shedding of the chrysalis a new chrysalis appears,—more tenuous, perhaps, more diaphanous, but woven of like tenuous material,—a mental and physical texture spun by Karma from the inherited illusions, passions, desires, pains and pleasures, of innumerable lives."

Nirvana was, then, the destruction of craving, and so release from rebirth: the ceasing of becoming. Yet it was not cessation, but emancipation: what Lafcadio Hearn called the passing of conditioned being into unconditioned being.

By Nirvana Gautama meant what Krishna meant by unity with Brahma and what Jesus meant by Eternal Life, or the Kingdom of Heaven. This is why Sir Edwin Arnold called Buddhism "the proudest assertion of human freedom," because in time all will reach Nirvana, although some will be delayed upon the journey through their wisdom being obscured.

Arnold's poem was based upon a work in the Pali Canon, *Lalitavistara,* a biography of Gautama. In the concluding pages he puts into the mouth of Gautama the exposition of the Law of Karma. It is too long to quote in full, but these verses perfectly express the teaching:

> *Pray not! the Darkness will not brighten! Ask*
> *Nought from the Silence, for it cannot speak!*
> *Vex not your mournful minds with pious pains!*
> *Ah! Brothers, Sisters! seek*
>
> *Nought from the helpless gods by gift and hymn,*
> *Nor bribe with blood, nor feed with fruits and cakes;*
> *Within yourselves deliverance must be sought;*
> *Each man his prison makes. . . .*

The Teaching of Gautama

Who toiled a slave may come anew a Prince
  For gentle worthiness and merit won;
Who ruled a King may wander earth in rags
  For things done and undone.

Only, while turns this wheel invisible,
  No pause, no peace, no staying-place can be;
Who mounts may fall, who falls will mount; the
    spokes
  Go round unceasingly! . . .

Ye suffer from yourselves. None else compels,
  None other holds you that ye live and die,
And whirl upon the wheel, and hug and kiss
  Its spokes of agony,

Its tire of tears, its nave of nothingness.
  Behold, I show you Truth! Lower than hell,
Higher than Heaven, outside the utmost stars,
  Farther than Brahm doth dwell,

Before beginning, and without an end,
  As space eternal and as surety sure,
Is fixed a Power divine which moves to good,
  Only its laws endure. . . .

It slayeth and it saveth, nowise moved
  Except upon the working out of doom;
Its threads are Love and Life; and Death and
      Pain
  The shuttles of its loom. . . .

It will not be contemned of any one;
  Who thwarts it loses, and who serves it gains;
The hidden good it pays with peace and bliss,
  The hidden ill with pains. . . .

It knows not wrath nor pardon; utter-true
  Its measures mete, its faultless balance weighs;
Times are as nought, to-morrow it will judge,
  Or after many days.

Buddha's favourite symbol was the lotus, and once he explained its significance:

"Just as the lotus, born of watery mud, grows in the water, rises above the water, and is not defiled by it: so have I arisen in the world, and passed beyond the world, and am not defiled by the world." For this reason he came to be represented standing or sitting upon a lotus pedestal in pictures and statues.

Since Gautama's death his teaching has endured in Asia, and even though it passed away from the land of his birth, modern Brahminism shows its influence, and its lessons are clearly seen in Hindu thought.

"More than a third of mankind," wrote Arnold, "owe their moral and religious ideas to this illustrious prince; whose personality, though imperfectly revealed in the existing sources of information, cannot but appear the highest, gentlest, holiest and most beneficent with one exception, in the history of Thought."

As I have tried to show in this brief analysis, Gautama's teaching was, in all essentials, the wisdom which five hundred years later Jesus returned to earth to teach: indeed, Gautama, in the one prophecy he is recorded to have made, seems to have foreseen the advent of Jesus when he told his disciples that the day would come when there would arise in the world one endowed with full enlightenment, a Buddha like himself, who should proclaim the ancient wisdom in all its purity.

And if Gautama's original teaching has, like

that of the other Great Masters, been distorted and even degraded by the priesthood into whose charge it was committed, it is the only religion which has shown itself at all times tolerant of other beliefs, as its Founder would have had it. Unlike Christianity, it has never been taught to others at the point of the sword, and alone among the great faiths of the world its record is unstained by blood.

SEVEN

The Teaching of Lao Tsze

Lao Tsze (or Tzŭ), the greatest of the Chinese philosophers, flourished about the time when Gautama was teaching in India. Little is known of the facts of his life, but that does not greatly matter, for enough of his teaching remains on record to show that he was in the line of the Great Masters who all taught the same wisdom.

Legend is woven about his name. One relates that he was born of a virgin who conceived him at

the sight of a falling star. Others have rendered
his name "Old Boy," because he is said to have
been born with a white beard: an example of
how legend grows from truth, since Lao Tsze was
indeed born old, but not in earth age: he was
an "old soul" who had been to earth so many
times that he was nearing the last incarnation.
Perhaps his name is best rendered "Venerable
Philosopher."

He is said to have been born in 604 B.C., in the
province of Honan, and was thus an elder contemporary of Confucius, with whom he had at
least one meeting. He became librarian at the
Court of Chow, the capital of Honan, but towards
the end of his life he gave up his appointment and
left the city by the gate of the royal domains near
the pass of Han-ku. According to the historical
records of Ssǔ-ma-Ch'ien (c. 100 B.C.), the war-
den of the gate, seeing that he was preparing to
withdraw himself from the world, asked him to set
down his teaching before he went. Lao Tsze
thereupon wrote an ethical treatise composed of

5,000 Chinese characters. Then he departed, and no man knows where he died.

His teaching is enshrined in the *Tao Tê Ching*, the authenticity of which many scholars deny, maintaining that it is an unauthorized compilation of his sayings, or even the forgery of a later age.

"It has been urged that we must make allowance here for Confucian bias," wrote Dr Lionel Giles in his introduction to *The Sayings of Lao Tzu;* "but the internal evidence alone should suffice to dispel the notion, to which many eminent sinologues have clung, that the *Tao Tê Ching* in its present form can possibly represent the actual work of Lao Tzu. On the other hand, it is highly probable that much of it is substantially what he said or wrote, though carelessly collected and pieced together at random. Ssǔ-ma-Ch'ien, who published his history in 91 B.C., and was consequently removed from Lao Tzu by a much longer period than we are from Shakespeare, tells us that the Sage wrote a book of five thousand and odd words; and, indeed, by that time the *Tao Tê Ching* may possibly have existed in something like its present shape. But anyone who reflects on the turbulent condition of China during the intervening centuries, and the chaotic state of primitive literature before the labours of Confucius, to say nothing of the Burning of the Books in 213 B.C., will find it hard to convince himself that Ssŭ-ma-Ch'ien ever had before him the actual writings of the philosopher."

Mr Arthur Waley, in *The Way and its Power*, goes even farther and declares, "We do not know and it is unlikely that we shall ever know who wrote the *Tao Tê Ching*"; and although he admits that the name of Lao Tsze has been connected with it for two thousand years, he considers him to have been a composite figure.

With deference to Mr Waley's scholarship, I prefer to accept the view that Lao Tsze was one of the Great Masters who taught the true wisdom, and that the *Tao Tê Ching*, whether in the form written by him or not, substantially represents his teaching, even though certain passages may be obscure, often owing to the conciseness of expression and the difficulty of framing the ideas he had to convey in a language which was still imperfectly developed.

So far as we know, Lao Tsze performed no miracles or acts of healing. In this he resembles Gautama. Like Jesus, he stressed the lessons of humility, which may thus have been the lesson he had returned to learn.

Referring to the ancient saying, "He who would be preserved entire must first be twisted," he taught that to become straight one must first allow oneself to be bent, to be filled one must first be empty, that he who has little shall presently have more, and that he who has much shall go astray. Wherefore the wise man does not show himself, and is seen everywhere; he does not boast, consequently he succeeds; he does not think overmuch on his work, consequently it endures; he strives with none, and thus none can strive with him.

Here is the teaching of the Law of Karma; and that of the Sermon on the Mount. And again, "To them that do good to me I return good. To them that do evil to me I return good. So all become good. With the faithful I would keep faith; with the unfaithful I would also keep faith, in order that they may become faithful. Even if a man is bad, how can it be right to cast him off? Requite iniquity with kindness." That is to say, by doing good to our enemies we put them in our debt, and so they must become good in order to repay that debt. So Jesus said, "Love your enemies, do good to them that hate you."

Lao Tsze taught that the strong must be content to be weak, and that the great must make lowliness their foundation. Even so a woman by quiescence overcomes a man, since quiescence is a form of humility.

"I have three treasures, which I prize," declared the Sage. "The first is sympathy; the second is frugality; the third is humility, which keeps me from putting myself before others. Only the gentle can be truly brave, only the frugal can be truly liberal; only the humble can become leaders of men." Like Jesus, he taught that "he who strives after tenderness can become even as a little child."

Compassion, he taught, brings victory to the attacker, and safety to the defender. The greatest conquerors are those who overcome their enemies without fighting, the greatest leaders those who yield place to others. "This is called the power of not striving, the capacity for directing men; it is being the compeer of heaven, the highest goal of the ancients."

This doctrine of inaction, apparently so at variance with the material conceptions of the West, is nevertheless akin to the teaching of Buddha and was eminently suitable for a race like the Chinese, for, as Lao Tsze put it, "The Empire has been preserved by letting things take their course." That is as true of China to-day as when Lao Tsze lived.

But Lao Tsze's conception of inaction was that of Gautama rather than our own. Lao Tsze did not recommend what a British statesman once described as "masterly inactivity," so much as consideration before action; that is, allowing intuition—or memory—to wait upon action, so that wisdom might come through.

"He who knows what God is and what man is,

has attained," said Lao Tsze. "Knowing what God is, he knoweth that man proceedeth therefrom, knowing what man is (i.e. body, soul and spirit) he rests in the knowledge of the known, waiting for the knowledge of the unknown."

"Who is there that can make muddy water clear?" he asked. "But if allowed to remain still, it will gradually become clear of itself." That is to say, how can wisdom come to a mind agitated by emotion? But if the mind is stilled, past experience will point the way clearly to right action.

Lao Tsze's teaching on war is the natural corollary of this doctrine. War is a calamity, and there is no greater disaster than to engage in it without good cause. Thorns and brambles grow in the wake of armies, and he who overcomes by violence will himself thus be overcome. The good general is he who stays his hand and does not boast of his victory; and the warrior who has slain many foes should bewail them rather than show elation at his own prowess.

Here is the mildness of Gautama, and again and again Lao Tsze preaches moderation and the

Middle Way, as Gautama did. He taught that extreme straightness was as bad as crookedness, extreme cleverness as bad as folly. The sword-edge which is over-tempered soon grows dull; the bow which is stretched too far may snap in two. The wise man must avoid excess, extravagance and display, for the things of earth are impermanent. That which was before will be behind, that which was hot will be cold, that which was strong will be weak, that which was whole will fall. Great ambitions entail great sacrifices, and hoarding brings naught but loss. Therefore he who knows when he has enough will not be put to shame, and he who knows when to stop will come to no harm.

Like those before him, Lao Tsze deplored an outward show of righteousness, and bade men be true to their own conscience, "to show simplicity, to embrace plain dealing, to reduce selfishness, to moderate desire."

Lao Tsze also laid stress upon the difference between wisdom and mere earth knowledge. Diffident as I feel to criticize so eminent a sinologue as Dr Giles, I am convinced that in one passage of his translation he has lost sight of this difference. "He who tries to govern a kingdom by his sagacity is of that kingdom the despoiler; but he who does not govern by sagacity is the kingdom's blessing." Read thus, the meaning of the passage is obscure, for surely sagacity, in the sense of acute mental discernment, is a good quality in a ruler. The Reverend James Legge, in his article on Lao Tsze in the *Encyclopaedia Britannica* translates this passage, "He who tries to govern a state by wisdom is a scourge to it, while he who does not try to govern it thereby is a blessing." Here is worse confusion still.

Mr Waley renders the passage entirely differently:

Those who seek to rule by giving knowledge
Are like bandits preying on the land.
Those who rule without giving knowledge
Bring a stock of good fortune to the land.

What Lao Tsze intended to convey, I suggest, was that a ruler must not depend on mere earth knowledge, or book-learning, but must govern with the wisdom and experience acquired in other lives. This is the meaning of the saying, as translated by Mr Waley: "True wisdom is different from much learning; much learning means little wisdom."

Although much of Lao Tsze's teaching, like that of Gautama, is on a high ethical plane, nevertheless it has a practical application to everyday affairs, as when he speaks of the ill feeling that inevitably remains after the settlement of a quarrel. To counteract this the wise man adheres to his obligations, but refrains from exacting fulfilment from others. "The man of integrity considers the spirit of the contract; the man without integrity considers only his claims."

And again, like Jesus, he taught the impermanence of the things of earth. "He who grasps more than he can hold, would be better without any. If a house is crammed with treasure of gold and jade, it will be impossible to guard them all." Finally, like every other great teacher, he taught that man must know himself: "Mighty is he who conquers himself."

So far as we know, Lao Tsze gave no teaching on the after-life, except in his saying, "When one dies, one is not lost; there is no other longevity." In his recorded words there is no direct mention of Reincarnation, although this saying (in Dr Giles's translation) is significant: "All things alike do their work, and then we see them subside. When they have reached their bloom, each returns to its origin. Returning to their origin means rest or fulfilment of destiny. This reversion is an eternal law. To know that law is to be enlightened. Not to know it, is misery and calamity. He who knows the eternal law is liberal-minded. Being liberal-minded, he is just. Being just, he is kingly. Being kingly, he is akin to Heaven. Being akin to Heaven, he possesses Tao. Possessed of Tao, he endures for ever. Though his body suffers, yet he suffers no harm."

Much of Lao Tsze's teaching shows that he had full knowledge of the Law of Karma. "Heaven's net is wide," he wrote. "Though its meshes are wide, it lets nothing slip through." He taught that if a man would contract he must first expand, that if he would weaken, he must first strengthen, that if he would overthrow he must first raise up, that if he would take he must first give. This he called the dawn of intelligence. We must sacrifice much to obtain great love, suffer great loss to obtain much treasure. He who prides himself on wealth and honour hastens his own downfall, he who strikes with a sharp point will not himself be safe for long, and he who raises himself on tiptoe cannot stand firm, while "the violent and stiff-necked die not by a natural death."

Lao Tsze looks at Nature and sees all things working silently and without display. "They come into being and possess nothing. They fulfil their functions and make no claim." Like the lilies of the field they toil not, neither do they spin. Therefore, warns the Sage, when you have acquired merit, make no claim for it, for if you make no claim it shall not be taken from you. "Follow diligently the way in your own heart, but make no display of it to the world. Remain behind, and you shall lead, remain without and you shall be within."

One of Lao Tsze's wisest sayings, completely in accordance with the Law of Karma, was that failure is the foundation of success, and the means by which it is achieved. Karma indeed teaches that success is attained only by training in many lives, wherein countless failures have been faced with courage, until attainment has come. "In the management of affairs," Lao Tsze said, "people constantly break down just when they are nearing success. Were they to take as much care at the end as at the beginning, they would not fail."

The expression Tao which occurs repeatedly in Lao Tsze's teaching, has been variously translated—Supreme Power, the Way, Reason, Nature, the Word, in the sense of the Greek Logos, the Path of Perfection, or as the equivalent of Plato's Idea of the Good. There are passages when it appears synonymous with Karma: "Tao takes from those who have abundance and gives to those who have too little," and "Tao is like the drawing of a bow: it brings down what is high and raises what is low;" and again, "Tao has no favourites. It gives to all good men without distinction." Nevertheless, Tao cannot be identified with Karma. "It means a road, path, way," says Mr Arthur Waley in *The Way and its Power*, "and hence, the way in which one does something; method, principle, doctrine. . . . Each school of philosophy had its *tao*, its doctrine of the way in which life should be ordered. Finally, in a particular school of philosophy whose followers ultimately came to be called Taoists, *tao* meant 'the way the universe works,' and ultimately, something very like God, in the more abstract and philosophical sense of that term." Thus it was not only a doctrine but "the ultimate reality in which all attributes are united."

Mr Waley points out that all the meaning-extensions of the word *tao* (even including the last: "I am the Way") also exist in European language. The word *tê* in *Tao Tê Ching* is more difficult, for although it is usually translated "virtue," it can have a bad connotation as well as a good one.

"On examining the history of the word," says Mr Waley, "we find that it means something much more like the Indian *Karma*, save that the fruits of *tê* are generally manifested here and now; whereas *karma* is bound up with a theory of transmigration, and its effects are not usually seen in this life, but in a subsequent incarnation. *Tê* is anything that happens to one or that one does of a kind indicating that, as a consequence, one is going to meet with good or bad luck. It means, so to speak, the stock of credit (or the deficit) that at any given moment a man has at the bank of fortune."

The word is also connected with the idea of planting and so of potentiality. Fields planted with corn represent potential riches, and thus *tê* means "a latent power, a 'virtue' inherent in something."

Perhaps the meaning of the word *Tao* may be best rendered "perfected knowledge," which is the equivalent of the ancient Egyptians' "moon wisdom," the moon being the symbol of pure wisdom. *Tê* is then the path, or the power, whereby that wisdom may be opened or attained: to be accomplished only by using the highest of oneself, the utmost memory that each possesses, so that enlightenment may come through. Thus *Tao Tê Ching* may be rendered "The Book of the Path to Perfected Knowledge."

Lao Tsze likened Tao to a vessel which gives water without ever needing to be filled, a deep pool which never dries. In it all sharpness is blunted, all knots are untied, all glare shaded, all unrest made still. Tranquillity of the spirit is the essence of Taoism, and, as Mr Waley says, to be in harmony with, not in rebellion against, the fundamental laws of the universe, is the first step on the way to Tao.

Lao Tsze found in China, just as Buddha found in India, a gross materialism. In China the prevailing religion was ancestor worship, the dead being propitiated by sacrificial rites. Prevailing doubt as to whether the dead, even if they could be said to exist beyond the grave, were conscious of affairs on earth, gave to the sacrifices of food and the libations of wine little significance beyond pretexts for social gatherings. A school of Hedonists arose, whose object was to get the best they could out of life, and an opposing school of Quietists, who wished to cleanse the heart by the stilling of all outward activities, so that one might work back through one's layers of materialism until Pure Consciousness was reached. Although Lao Tsze never taught, or intended to teach the masses, he rendered the Chinese attitude of mind receptive to the spread of Buddhism which was to sweep China in later years.

Lao Tsze's teaching in its most spiritual form was not a way of life for ordinary men and women, any more than the esoteric doctrine of Buddha and Jesus: but he who had ears might hear and accept. As Mr Waley points out, the author of the *Tao Tê Ching* did but teach what others had taught before him, but he adapted and wove together into a harmonious pattern accepted proverbs and maxims and the aphorisms of older Taoists just as Jesus was to do five hundred years later, by his own wisdom enhancing their spiritual appeal.

To Lao Tsze, Tao is the sanctuary where all things find refuge, the treasure of the good man, and the guardian and saviour of him who is not good. Here Tao is one with "conscience," if we can admit that conscience is the memory of all wisdom gathered in all our lives. Right action in all circumstances is the achievement of Tao. If Tao is obscured, then right action is obscured. By attaining oneness with Tao—or listening to the dictates of conscience, the highest a man knows—one becomes above either favour or disgrace, benefits or injuries, honour or contempt: and is therefore esteemed above all mankind.

"Why was it that the man of old esteemed this Tao so highly?" asked Lao Tsze. "Is it not because it may be daily sought and found, and can remit the sins of the guilty? Hence it is the most precious thing under Heaven."

Lao Tsze was writing five centuries before the Christian era. Yet his references to the wisdom of "the men of old" shows a recognition of great teachers before him. Indeed, he describes these "skilful philosophers" as subtle, spiritual, profound, penetrating, shrinking, like one who fords a stream in winter; cautious, like one who fears an attack from any quarter; circumspect, like a strange guest; self-effacing, like ice about to melt; simple, like unpolished wood. Whence, then, came the revelation of the wisdom which he taught, so close to what Gautama was then teaching in India, and Pythagoras in Greece? How else but through the memory of wisdom learned in other lives, and, in his present existence, by contact with those away from earth, dwelling on planes which his consciousness had been trained to reach. This was the ecstasy which he himself called Faraway Wandering. Another Chinese philosopher, Chuang Tzû, calls it "Wanderings alone with Tao in the Great Wilderness," and Mr Waley describes it as "not external journeys, but explorations of oneself, back to 'the Beginning of Things.'"

"When the day of revelation comes," wrote L. Adams Beck, in one of her loveliest short stories, "The Sea of Lilies," "it will be found how much of the religious thought of the divided faiths can be traced to common sources in an antiquity so vast that it strikes the soul with awe. May that knowledge bring union and surcease to the petty wranglings and contempts which cloud the living waters of Truth."

As with the teaching of every other Great Master, Lao Tsze's was not immune from those petty wranglings and contempts. Whereas the teaching of Krishna, Gautama and Jesus was obscured by the dogma of those who came after them, the lessons of Lao Tsze were destined, to use Dr Giles's words, "to be dragged into the mire of degrading superstition, which for centuries has made Taoism a byword of reproach." This magic and ritual was grafted on to Lao Tsze's teaching soon after his death and was apparent in the work of his earliest followers of whom there is record. Three centuries after his death Taoism had become a search for the fairy islands of the eastern sea where the herb of eternal life was to be found. When Buddhism first obtained a hold in China, in the second half of the first century, Taoism took the form of a recognized religion, with temples, monasteries, ritual and forms of public worship. Since then alchemy, geomancy and spiritualism have been associated with it, and modern Taoism is a system of wildest polytheism, so that, as Mr Legge says, Lao Tsze should not have to bear the obloquy of being its founder.

As it is, the ethics of Confucius have survived much closer to their original form than the teaching of Lao Tsze: perhaps because Confucius kept his feet planted on the earth, while Lao Tsze soared to the stars. In Maurice Magré's *Confucius and his Quest*, there is a penetrating exposition of the two men's ideals and an imaginative reconstruction of their traditional meeting. Confucius explained his plans for winning man to righteousness and for reviving old traditions, and bringing about a regime of justice and moderation. Lao Tsze shook his head in disapproval. What then, demanded Confucius, was the aim of life?

"The attainment of the path of perfection," was the reply.

Confucius asked by what means that path might be attained.

"Through immobility," he was told.

"Then am I wrong in wishing men to be ruled by justice?" demanded Confucius.

"It is not other men one must rule, but oneself," said Lao Tsze.

Confucius, the priest of mediocrity, departed, having found the atmosphere breathed by Lao Tsze too rarefied for his mundane mind. But later, when he had become a minister, he had a dream that he was flying with Lao Tsze. The wings of the Venerable Philosopher were immense, Confucius's infinitely smaller.

"I am afraid of falling!" he murmured, as they soared above the clouds. "We are too high!"

"One is never too high," said Lao Tsze. "The sky is boundless. Be animated by the desire to rise, and your wings will grow larger."

Confucius protested that he felt them growing smaller every moment, and, looking anxiously over his shoulder, saw that only a few bedraggled feathers remained.

"Cease thinking of the earth, and you will find the Path of Perfection," exhorted Lao Tsze.

"Never! I shall not renounce the earth that I love," shouted Confucius with all his might, and fell, while Lao Tsze continued to soar high above him.

Thus, with wit, perception, and a wholly admirable economy of criticism, M. Magré presents the philosophy of the two sages.

EIGHT

The Teaching
in the New Testament

People sometimes ask, if Reincarnation be true, why did not Jesus teach it? Perhaps the answer is that he had no need to teach it explicitly, since all his listeners believed in it and took it as a matter of course. For example, the followers of Mithra believed in Reincarnation; so did the Essenes, a secret society which had been in existence for thousands of years. Certainly there is nothing either in Reincarnation or the Law of Karma which is inconsistent with his teaching, and in his recorded sayings there are references to both.

Of John the Baptist he said, "If ye will receive it, this is Elias, which was for to come" (*Matthew, xi*, 14); and "Elias is come already, and they knew him not, but have done unto him whatsoever they listed." (*Matthew, xvii*, 12; *also Mark, ix*, 13). What possible meaning can either of these sayings have but that John was a reincarnation of the prophet Elias? It must be presumed that Jesus would not have spoken as he did unless his disciples had been familiar with the idea of Reincarnation, since he offers no explanation but makes two plain statements of fact.

Then, again, his question "Who do men say that I am?" suggests that he asked who the people believed him to have been in a previous life, and the suggestion is confirmed by the disciples' answer that he was either Elias or Jeremias, an answer which he neither refuted nor confirmed.

Then there is his saying, "Though I bear record of myself, yet my record is true: for I know whence I came and whither I go." (*John, viii*, 14).

This, I suggest, is the statement of a Master who, being able to reach planes away from earth, knew the truth of his past lives and the purpose of the journey. That he had this knowledge is shown by the words: "Your father Abraham rejoiced to see my day: and he saw it, and was glad. . . . Verily, verily. I say unto you, Before Abraham was, I am," (*John, viii*, 56, 58).

His much discussed saying, "I bring not peace but the sword" is not to be interpreted only as a fight against the forces of evil and the dogma of the Jewish religion, but implies that he did not teach what was easy and comfortable for ordinary men, but what was hard; he showed the personal discomfort of working off karma quickly—and the ultimate benefits to be gained thereby: "Till heaven and earth pass, one jot or one tittle shall in no wise pass from the law, till all be fulfilled." (*Matthew, v*, 18). What law? Not the law of the scribes and Pharisees, but the Law of Karma. Again, what can "the wages of sin is death" mean but that the karma for evil-doing entails returning to earth to suffer mortality until the sinner has learned his lessons? The ancient Egyptians were accustomed to regard life on earth as so inhibiting that they called it death, and what we call death was known to them as life.

Jesus expounded the main principles of his teaching in the Sermon on the Mount, to which, as I have shown, there are close parallels in the teaching of Krishna, Buddha and Lao Tsze. A life lived in accordance with the Law of Karma would embody both the beatitudes and the woes of the Sermon. Kindness, humility, tolerance, forgiveness, living without undue preoccupation with the things of earth, or worry about material affairs, and man's simple duty not only to his immediate associates but to all humanity: these Jesus taught. "Therefore all things whatsoever ye would that men should do to you, do ye even so to them," *(Matthew, vii, 12)* is the first principle of the Law of Karma.

Jesus taught that those who are merciful shall obtain mercy, that those who hunger shall be filled, that those who weep now shall presently laugh. He showed that to refrain from exacting an eye for an eye or a tooth for a tooth brought its own reward: "For if ye forgive men their trespasses, your heavenly Father will also forgive you." (*Matthew, vi,* 14). That man should love his enemies was the teaching not only of Jesus, but of Krishna, of Buddha, of Lao Tsze—"For if ye love them which love you, what reward have ye? do not even the publicans the same?" (*Matthew, v,* 46).

Jesus expressed the law of cause and effect when he said, "Give, and it shall be given unto you; good measure, pressed down, and shaken together, and running over, shall men give unto your bosom. For with the same measure that ye mete withal it shall be measured to you again." (*Luke, vi,* 38). And again, "He that is greatest among you shall be your servant. And whosoever shall exalt himself shall be abased; and he that shall humble himself shall be exalted." (*Matthew, xxiii,* 11–12). How would that be possible on the premise of a single existence? Then there is Krishna's injunction against doing good that good may come; and against making a parade of religion; and the same glorious promise: "Ask, and it shall be given you;

seek, and ye shall find; knock, and it shall be opened unto you." (*Matthew, vii,* 7).

Like Lao Tsze, the chief lesson which Jesus taught was humility. Even so, he could be uncompromising in his attitude to tyranny, oppression and unfair dealing, as when he drove the money-lenders from the Temple, and as in his injunction, "Give not that which is holy unto the dogs, neither cast ye your pearls before swine, lest they trample them under their feet, and turn again and rend you." (*Matthew, vii,* 6).

Further evidence that Jesus's teaching implied recognition of the Law of Karma is to be found in his acts of healing. In the case of the impotent man, his words "Behold, thou art made whole: sin no more, lest a worse thing come unto thee," (*John, v,* 14) seems to imply that both Jesus and his patient knew that the affliction was the result of karma; and so Jesus was warning him that unless he profited by experience and refrained from repeating the sin which had made it necessary for him to suffer, he would have to face the karmic result again, possibly in the shape of enhanced pain, since he would have deliberately closed his ears to his conscience.

In the case of the man blind from birth (*John, ix*, 1–7), the disciples' question, "Master, who did sin, this man, or his parents, that he was born blind?" clearly shows their belief in Reincarnation. They wished to know whether it was the karma of the man's parents to have a blind son, or whether the man was afflicted with blindness in adjustment of some fault committed in a previous life: for, since the man had been born blind, his affliction could not have been the result of anything he had done in his present life. It may be noted that Jesus accepted this question as a perfectly normal one, without rebuke.

Finally there is his saying to Nicodemus, "Except a man be born again, he cannot see the kingdom of God." (*John, iii*, 3). Here is a literal and plain statement of man's need to pass through life after life until he can reach spiritual attainment. The orthodox explanation is that the words "be born again" are to be interpreted "renewed in mind," but there seems no reason why we should not accept these words in their literal meaning, as, no doubt, Nicodemus did.

The concluding hours of Jesus's life upon earth, as recorded in the Gospels, show that he knew the karma he must undergo before his spirit could be free of earth. He acknowledged that it must be so, and he knew that one of his disciples must be the instrument of Karma: "The Son of man goeth as it is written of him: but woe unto that man by whom the Son of man is betrayed!" (*Matthew, xxvi,* 24). And in that scene in the Garden of Gethsemane, which shows so poignantly how even a Great Master must suffer while still in the thraldom of his physical body, he faced the karma that he knew was to be his greatest test. Exceeding sorrowful as his soul was, even unto death, he trembled at the physical suffering before him, perhaps even more at the humiliation and lowering of his pride, and his apprehension wrung from him the cry to his own Master, "If it be possible, let this cup pass from me." Then, the weakness past, courage triumphed gloriously and will once more controlled emotion: "Nevertheless not as I will, but as thou wilt;" and the final acceptance of adjustment, "If this cup may not pass away from me, except I drink it, thy will be done."

That submission was the more complete because he knew that, had he chosen, as for a moment he was perhaps tempted to choose, he had enough power to destroy those who were on their way to take him: yet when they confronted him he was resolute again. He warned the loyal disciple who smote off the ear of the high priest's servant, "All they that take the sword shall perish with the sword," and reproved him with the words, "The cup which my Father hath given me, shall I not drink it?" Even then, his humanity was proved by that last dreadful cry that was wrung from his tortured body, "My God, my God, why hast thou forsaken me?" But a little later he could say "Father, into thy hands I commend my spirit."

St Paul, whose part was to expound the teaching of Jesus, clearly believed in Reincarnation. I have already quoted the saying that is the epitome of the Law of Karma: "Be not deceived; God is not mocked: for whatsoever a man soweth, that shall he also reap," but the verses which follow (*Galatians, vi*, 8–9) go farther: "He that soweth to his flesh shall of the flesh reap corruption; but he that soweth to the Spirit shall of the Spirit reap life everlasting. And let us not be weary in well doing: for in due season we shall reap, if we faint not." And again, in II Corinthians, ix, 6–7, "He which soweth sparingly shall reap also sparingly; and he which soweth bountifully shall reap also bountifully. Every man according as he purposeth in his heart so let him give." Here is the whole teaching of the Law, and the corollary of the first saying is equally true: "Whatsoever a man reapeth, that hath he also sown."

In the second verse of the same chapter of Galatians the words "Bear ye one another's burdens" seem to demand the sense "Bear ye *with* one another's burdens." No one can assume responsibility for another's karma, though he may, and should, sympathize and help in another's trouble; and St Paul himself goes on to say, "Let every man prove his own work, and then shall he have rejoicing in himself alone, and not in another. For every man shall bear his own burden."

Here St Paul makes a point which is necessary to bear in mind when trying to help those in trouble. That they have earned that trouble we cannot doubt, if we believe in Karma; we know that they are being called upon to face suffering to adjust a previous wrong. If we identify ourselves too closely with that trouble we may do them harm, since we may deprive them of their opportunity of gaining experience and strengthening character. That does not mean we are not to help them, by giving them strength and courage. When a child has a difficult sum to do, it will profit him nothing if a doting parent sits down and does it for him; but if he is shown where he has gone wrong, and encouraged to work out the sum again, he may then be able to grasp something he had not understood before. Each one, whether child or grown man or woman, must fight his own battle and learn to stand alone. In this matter love and affection can prove unwisely overfond, and by the helper taking too much upon himself he will but weaken the character which needs more strength. The batteners and clingers of this world, especially if they be women, will usually find people who, in kindness of heart, will do their work for them, but they have still to learn that, having shirked the issue, they will have to face it again elsewhere, when they may find it even harder than before, until each learns the pride of achievement by his own efforts, and has "rejoicing in himself alone and not in another."

St Paul makes a direct reference to Reincarnation in Romans, ix, 10–14: "When Rebecca also had conceived by one, even by our father Isaac: (For the children being not yet born, neither having done any good or evil . . .) It was said unto her, The elder shall serve the younger. As it is written, Jacob have I loved, but Esau have I hated. What shall we say then? Is there unrighteousness with God? God forbid."

This statement has no meaning unless it refers to pre-existence, since God could not have either loved or hated Rebecca's children before they were born.

So, too, with the doctrine of original sin, as expounded by St Paul, with which all mankind, descended from fallen Adam, are held to be universally infected from their conception and birth. But since the essence of sin is the motive to do wrong, how can a baby newly born into the world be responsible for acts except those committed in a previous life?

Commenting on these passages, Chevalier Ramsay says: "If it be said that these texts are obscure, that pre-existence is only drawn from them by induction, and that this opinion is not revealed in Scripture by express words, I answer that the doctrines of the immortality of the soul are nowhere revealed in the sacred oracles of the Old or New Testament, but because all the morals and doctrines are founded upon these great truths. We may say the same of pre-existence. The doctrine is nowhere expressly revealed, but it is evidently supposed, as without it original sin becomes not only inexplicable, but absurd, repugnant, and impossible."

In the first Epistle of St Peter (*i*, 22–3) the exhortation "See that ye love one another with a pure heart fervently: Being born again, not of corruptible seed, but of incorruptible, by the word of God, which liveth and abideth for ever," suggests the return of the spirit to earth, while the promise in Revelations (*iii*, 12) "Him that overcometh will I make a pillar in the temple of my God, and he shall go no more out," seems to allude to the spirit which has benefited by every experience and so has no further need to return to earth. In a later chapter (*xiii*, 10), the words "He that leadeth into captivity shall go into captivity: he that killeth with the sword must be killed with the sword," is also the teaching of Karma.

It may be contended that it is easy to pick out isolated passages from the scriptures and to interpret them in a desired sense to prove a case. But in those which I have quoted, the natural sense seems to imply a belief in Reincarnation and Karma, even though the orthodox authorities would not care to admit that possibility. What cannot be denied, however, is that the early

Christian Church, and most of the Christian Fathers, including Origen and St Augustine (who believed Plotinus to be a reincarnation of Plato), accepted Reincarnation, which was declared a heresy by the Council of Constantinople in the year 551, possibly on account of its connection with Greek philosophy on the one hand and Jewish tradition on the other. Origen's master, Clemens Alexandrinus, taught Reincarnation as a divine tradition authorized by St Paul.

Origen, following Pythagoras and Plato, maintained that every soul comes into the world "strengthened by the victories or weakened by the defeats of its previous life." Its place in its new incarnation was determined by its previous actions, good or ill, and its work on earth decided its place in the life to follow; and Origen believed in the conception of ultimate reunion of spirit, when "the sons of God . . . shall be gathered into one, having fulfilled their duties in this world."

Later, according to Jerome, the doctrine was taught only to an esoteric few. Nevertheless, as Walker mentions in his book *Reincarnation,*

"Many of the orthodox Church Fathers welcomed Reincarnation as a ready explanation of the fall of man and the mystery of life, and distinctly preached it as the only means of reconciling the existence of suffering with a merciful God. It was an essential part of the Church philosophy for many centuries in the rank and file of Christian thought, being stamped with the authority of the leading thinkers of Christendom, and then gradually was frowned upon as the Western influence predominated, until it became heresy, and at length survived only in a few scattered sects."

Schopenhauer, reviewing the belief in Reincarnation as revealed in the Vedas, the sacred books of India, in Brahmanism and Buddhism, in the Greek mysteries (as shown in the ninth book of Plato's Laws), in the Edda, and as the foundation of the religion of the Druids, said:

"What resists this belief is Judaism, together with the two religions which have sprung from it, because they teach the creation of man out of nothing, and they have the hard task of linking on to this belief an endless existence *a parte post.*

They certainly have succeeded, with fire and sword, in driving out of Europe and part of Asia that consoling primitive belief of mankind; it is still doubtful for how long. Yet how difficult this was is shown by the oldest Church histories. Most of the heretics were attached to this belief; for example, Simonists, Basilidians, Valentinians, Marrionists, Gnostics, and Manicheans. . . . Even the passage of the Bible (*Matthew, xvi*, 13–15) only obtains a rational meaning if we understand it as spoken under the assumption of the dogma of metempsychosis. . . . In Christianity, however, the doctrine of original sin, i.e. the doctrine of punishment for the sins of another individual, has taken the place of the transmigration of souls, and the expiation in this way of all the sins committed in an earlier life. Both identify the existing man with one who has existed before: the transmigration of souls does so directly, original sin indirectly."

In the preceding chapters I have tried to show not only that the Great Masters, Krishna, Buddha, Lao Tsze and Jesus accepted the Law of Karma and Reincarnation, but also that their teaching, founded on identical principles, offered to mankind not (as commonly supposed) four distinct sets of ethical principles or aspects of God, but one single all-embracing wisdom, founded on eternal truth, and derived not from their own conceptions but from the same source of divine revelation, "the highest pinnacle to which man can attain." If mankind could but have understood this unity of teaching in the past, and if it could have regarded the beliefs of others as facets of the same great jewel and not the glitter of imitation stones, the world's history might have been written differently. But at least it is not too late for us to reach this understanding: that every great teacher who has come to earth has taught the same lessons of gentleness and moderation, which may be embodied in the two sayings, "Do unto others as ye would they should do unto you" and "Love thy neighbour as thyself."

NINE

Great Men
on Reincarnation and Karma

Although Herodotus reported the ancient Egyptians' belief in Reincarnation, Pythagoras was the first of the Greeks to teach the doctrine. Pythagoras believed that, in an earlier life, Mercury had given him the power to remember his previous incarnations. He claimed to have been a Trojan named Euphorbus, who had been fatally wounded by Menelaus at the siege of Troy. Then he had been reborn as Hermotimus, and, on entering a temple of Apollo, he pointed out the shield of Eu-phorbus, which Menelaus had sent to the temple as a dedicatory offering: by that time so rusted away that nothing remained but the carved ivory face upon the boss. Before reincarnating as Pythagoras he declared that he had been a fisher-man of Delos.

Pythagoras held that a man might reincarnate in some body other than human, on which Hiero-cles, with greater knowledge, commented that the human soul could not transmigrate into the form of a beast or a plant, since it must be impossible for the soul to change its essential being, and, once human, it must remain so.

It might well be that Plato was a reincarnation of Pythagoras. Plato drew up a list of the various conditions of life for the various "ranks" of soul, that of an autocratic monarch ranking lowest of all. In the tenth book of *The Laws*, he taught that those who led just lives in the conditions ap-pointed them would afterwards receive a better lot, while those who lived unjustly would fare worse, and in every succession of life and death each man "will do and suffer what like may fitly suffer at the hands of like."

Among the Romans, Cicero, puzzled by the mistakes and suffering of human life, came to the conclusion that the philosophers of old had "some glimpses of the truth when they said that men are born in order to suffer the penalty for sins committed in a former life"—and, he might have added, to reap the benefit of their good deeds.

Virgil, in the sixth book of the *Aeneid*, describes Aeneas walking beside the River Lethe with Anchises, into whose mouth he puts the explanation that those who throng the banks are the spirits who are about to be born again, waiting to drink the waters of oblivion, so that, forgetful of past failure and disappointment, they may return to earth with fresh hope and courage: here is a lovely thought, to be considered by those who deny the possibility of Reincarnation because they have no memory of former lives. Ovid appears to have accepted the teaching that the human spirit could revert to the animal or plant world, but in

Metamorphoses he puts into the mouth of Pythagoras a beautiful passage on death and Reincarnation. I quote from Dryden's translation:

Those I would teach; and by right reason bring
To think of death as but an idle thing.
Why thus affrighted at an empty name,
A dream of darkness, and fictitious flame?
Vain themes of wit, which but in poems pass,
And fables of a world that never was?
What feels the body when the soul expires,
By time corrupted, or consumed by fires?
Nor dies the spirit, but new life repeats
In other form, and only changes seats. . . .
Then death, so call'd, is but old matter dress'd
In some new figure, and a varied vest:
Thus all things are but alter'd, nothing dies;
And here and there the unbodied spirit flies,
By time, or force, or sickness dispossess'd,
And lodges, where it lights, in man or beast;
Or hunts without, till ready limbs it find,
And actuates those according to their kind;
From tenement to tenement though toss'd,
The soul is still the same, the figure only lost:

And, as the soften'd wax new seals receives,
This face assumes, and that impression leaves;
Now call'd by one, now by another name,
The form is only changed, the wax is still the
     same.
So death, so call'd, can but the form deface;
The immortal soul flies out in empty space,
To seek her fortune in some other place.

Plutarch believed in Reincarnation, and Plotinus held that the soul, having expiated its sins in the darkness of the infernal regions, passed into new bodies, to gain fresh experience: the gods in their providence allotted to each individual in his successive lives a destiny in harmony with his past conduct. Those who had exercised their intellectual faculties reincarnated as human beings, but those who had lived only to gratify their senses entered the bodies of gluttonous animals. Those who had degraded their senses by disuse were compelled to vegetate as plants, while those who had loved music to excess reincarnated into the bodies of melodious birds. Those who had ruled tyrannically became eagles. One who had acquired civic virtues would return in a man's body, otherwise he might be transformed into a bee. To this teaching Hierocles's comments on Pythagoras apply, but Plotinus saw clearly when he said: "The experience of evil produces a clearer knowledge of good . . . for every soul possesses something which inclines towards the body, and something which tends upwards towards intellect." Indeed, so deeply did the luminous philosophy of Plotinus impress St Augustine that he was prepared to believe him to be the reincarnation of Plato.

Shakespeare has more than one reference to Pythagoras, for example in "The Merchant of Venice," when he makes Gratiano say to Shylock:

Thou almost mak'st me waver in my faith,
To hold opinion with Pythagoras,
That souls of animals infuse themselves
Into the trunks of men,

but he states the case for Reincarnation more clearly and more beautifully in Sonnet LIX:

If there be nothing new, but that which is
　　Hath been before, how are our brains beguil'd
Which, labouring for invention, bear amiss
　　The second burthen of a former child!
O, that record could with a backward look,
　　Even of five hundred courses of the sun,
Show me your image in some antique book,
　　Since mind at first in character was done.
That I might see what the old world could say
　　To this composed wonder of your frame;
Whe'er we are mended, or whe'er better they,
　　Or whether revolution be the same.
O, sure I am, the wits of former days
To subjects worse have given admiring praise.

John Donne, singing the progress of

　　　　a deathless soul,
Whom fate, which God made, but doth not
　　　　control,
Placed in most shapes,

wrote:

For though through many straits and lands I roam,
I launch at Paradise, and I sail towards home;

The course I there began shall here be stag'd,
Sails hoisted there, struck here, and anchors laid
In Thames, which were at Tigris and Euphrates
      weigh'd.

Milton's lines "On the Death of a Fair Infant" seek to solve the problem of that brief return to earth:

Wert thou some star, which from the ruined roof,
Of shaked Olympus by mischance didst fall;
Which careful Jove in nature's true behoof
Took up, and in fit place did re-instal?
Or did of late earth's sons besiege the wall
   Of sheeny Heaven, and thou some goddess fled
Among us here below to hide thy nectared head?

Or wert thou that just maid who once before
Forsook the hated earth, oh! tell me sooth,
And camest again to visit us once more?
Or wert thou that sweet-smiling youth?
Or that crowned matron, sage white-robèd Truth?
   Or any other of that heavenly brood
Let down in cloudy throne to do the world some
      good?

Or wert thou of the golden-wingèd host,
Who, having clad thyself in human weed,
To earth from thy prefixèd seat didst post,
And after short abode fly back with speed,
As if to show what creatures Heaven doth breed;
Thereby to set the hearts of men on fire
To scorn the sordid world, and unto Heaven
aspire?

The same idea inspired Dryden's "Ode to the Memory of Mrs Anne Killigrew":

If thy pre-existing soul
Was form'd at first with myriads more,
It did through all the mighty poets roll
Who Greek or Latin laurels wore,
And was that Sappho last, which once it was
before.

Goethe pictured the soul of man like water, coming from heaven and mounting thither, to return to earth again, forever changing.

"Why has fate linked us so closely to each other?" he wrote to Frau von Stein. For him the only answer was that she had been his sister or his wife; and the memory of that truth of old was forever with him.

Lessing believed that every individual man—one sooner, another later—travels the same way by which the race reaches its perfection. Not in one life: but why should not every man have existed more than once? Was the hypothesis so laughable, he asked, because it was the oldest? Why should he himself not return to earth so long as he was capable of acquiring fresh knowledge and experience? Did one throw away so much from one life that there was nothing to repay the trouble of return? Was that a reason against it? Or because one forgot one had been here before? Happy for man that he did forget, for the recollection of his former life would but cause him to make poor use of the present.

Schopenhauer declared that if an Asiatic asked him for a definition of Europe he would answer that it was that part of the world that was haunted by the incredible delusion that man's present birth was his first entrance into life. The doctrine of metempsychosis, he maintained, sprang from the earliest and noblest ages of earth, and had always been present in the world as the belief of the great majority of the human race. He held that death meant rest for the will, as sleep for the individual, and that through Lethe, the sleep of death, the will flung off the memory of its sufferings and reappeared refreshed and refitted as a new being, ready to attempt new shores. He maintained that every new-born being came fresh to a new existence, but contained the indestructible seed out of which that existence had risen. The persons who were closest to us in one life would be born with us in the next, and have the same or similar sentiments to us as now, whether friendly or hostile.

So, too, Nietzsche held that man's duty was present with him every instant, and that he must live so that he might desire to live again. It must needs be that we should live again, since we had already existed times without number, and all things with us. "How could I not be ardent for Eternity," he cried, "and for the marriage ring of rings—the Ring of Return?"

It would of course be dangerous to impute beliefs to a dramatist or a novelist because he put certain opinions into the mouths of his characters. But it is worth noticing that in *Emperor and Galilean*, Ibsen made Maximus bid Julian consider whether he were not Alexander born again, not, as before, in immaturity, but perfectly equipped for the fulfilment of the test. Maximus propounds the theory that there is One who ever reappears, at certain intervals, in the course of human history. Who knows, he asks, how often he has wandered among us when none have recognized him, and he suggests that Julian himself may once have been in the Galilean whom he now persecutes.

Many of French writers and philosophers believed in Reincarnation. Voltaire declared that it was not more surprising to be born twice than once, since everything in Nature is resurrection. Balzac held that a lifetime might be needed merely to gain the virtues which adjust the errors of a man's preceding life: those virtues, slowly developing, were the invisible links which bind each of man's existences to the others—existences which the spirit alone remembers, since matter has no memory for spiritual things. Thought, he insisted in *Seraphita*, alone held to tradition of the byegone life.

In *Consuelo*, George Sand evolved that strange character Albert, who could remember his previous incarnations and, when asked how he had been able to learn so many languages, replied that he knew them before he was born, and that he had only to recall them to memory. In the dramatic scene where he takes leave of his sister, he begs her to become joined to him by the marriage vow, so that they may be reunited in their next lives, and he be reborn calm and strong, free from the memory of past lives which had been his torment and punishment for so many centuries.

Victor Hugo, in *Life and Death*, made this noble profession of faith: "I am a soul. I know well that what I shall render up to the grave is not myself. That which is myself will go elsewhere. Earth, thou art not my abyss!" He explained that a man might dream that he was a lion, a bird or a serpent. He awoke to find himself a man. So with all the earthly lives he had to live: the ego which persists after the awakening from a dream is the ego which existed before and after it. The ego which persisted after death existed before and after life.

"Once accept the theory of pre-existence," wrote André Pezzani, "and a glorious light is thrown on the dogma of sin, for it becomes the result of personal faults from which the guilty soul must be purified." Jean Reynaud expressed the same belief when he said, "Let us banish the idea of disorder from the earth, by opening the gates of time beyond our birth, as we have banished the idea of injustice by opening other gates beyond the tomb"; and Allan Kardec gave a lucid exposition of Karma when he suggested that material life was a sort of filter, or alembic, through which a man must pass many times before he could attain perfection.

"To every awakened soul comes the question, 'Why does evil exist?'" said Pascal. So long as it remained unsolved, suffering remained a threatening Sphinx. The key to the secret lay, he believed, in evolution—by which he meant spiritual evolution—which could be accomplished only by Reincarnation. Once man learned that suffering is the necessary result of divine manifestation, that inequalities are due to the varying stages which men and women have reached, that although slave of the past he is master of the future, and that, finally, the same glorious goal awaits all, then despair would cease to be, hatred, envy and rebellion would have fled away, and peace would reign over a humanity made wise by knowledge.

Of great Americans, Benjamin Franklin was the first to proclaim his belief in Reincarnation. Seeing that God wasted nothing, not even a drop of water, he could not believe in the annihilation of souls, or imagine that God would waste millions of existing minds and put himself to the continual trouble of making new ones. Thus, finding himself existing in the world, he believed that he would, in some shape or other, always exist; and he added, "With all the inconveniences human life is liable to, I shall not object to a new edition of mine, hoping, however, that the *errata* of the last may be corrected." The same thought is expressed in the epitaph he wrote for himself at the age of 23. Although so well known, it is worth quoting:

The body
of
Benjamin Franklin,
Printer,
Like the cover of an old book,
Its contents worn out,
And stripped of its lettering and gilding,
Lies here, food for worms.
But the work shall not be lost,
For it will, as he believed, appear once more,
In a new and more elegant edition,
Revised and corrected
by
The Author.

"We must infer our destiny from the preparation," wrote Emerson. "We are driven by instinct to have innumerable experiences which are of no visible value, and we may revolve through many lives before we shall assimilate or exhaust them. Now there is nothing in nature capricious, or whimsical, or accidental, or unsupported. Nature never moves by jumps, but always in steady and supported advances. . . . If there is the desire to live, and in larger sphere, with more knowledge and power, it is because life and power are good for us, and we are the natural depositories of these gifts. The love of life is out of all proportion to the value set on a single day, and seems to indicate a conviction of immense resources and possibilities proper to us, on which we have never drawn. All the comfort I have found teaches me to confide that I shall not have less in times and places that I do not yet know."

In Walt Whitman's "Song of Myself" the poet asserts, nobly and courageously, his belief in Reincarnation:

I know I am deathless,
I know this orbit of mine cannot be swept by a
    carpenter's compass. . . .
And whether I come to my own to-day or in ten
    thousand or ten million years,

I can cheerfully take it now, or with equal cheer-
fulness I can wait.
My foothold is tenon'd and mortis'd in granite,
I laugh at what you call dissolution,
And I know the amplitude of time. . . .
I do not despise you priests, all time, all the
world over,
My faith is the greatest of faiths and the least of
faiths,
Enclosing worship ancient and modern and all
between ancient and modern,
Believing I shall come again upon the earth after
five thousand years. . . .
Births have brought us richness and variety,
And other births will bring us richness and
variety. . . .
I am an acme of things accomplished, and I am
an encloser of things to be.

Turning to English writers of the eighteenth and nineteenth centuries and after, I find that David Hume made this logical pronouncement in favour of Reincarnation: "What is corruptible must also be ungenerable. The soul, therefore, if immortal, existed before our birth. . . . Metempsychosis is therefore the only system of this kind that philosophy can hearken to."

Huxley considered that "In the doctrine of transmigration, whatever its origin, Brahminical and Buddhist speculation found, ready to hand, the means of constructing a plausible vindication of the ways of the Cosmos to man. . . . This plea of justification is not less plausible than others; and none but very hasty thinkers will reject it on the ground of inherent absurdity. Like the doctrine of evolution itself, that of transmigration has its roots in the world of reality; and it may claim such support as the great argument from analogy is capable of supplying."

Walter Scott had no such definite belief, yet he was not insensible to the possibility of Reincarnation. He records how, at dinner time on the evening of February 16, 1828, he was haunted by the sense of pre-existence—"A confused idea that nothing that passed was said for the first time.

That the same topics had been discussed, and the same persons had stated the same opinions on them." This sensation, so familiar to us all, he referred to again in a passage in *Guy Mannering*:

"Why is it that some scenes awaken thoughts which belong, as it were, to dreams of early and shadowy recollections, such as old Brahmin moonshine would have ascribed to a state of previous existence? How often do we find ourselves in society which we have never before met, and yet feel impressed with a mysterious and ill-defined consciousness that neither the scene nor the speakers nor the subject are entirely new; nay, feel as if we could anticipate that part of the conversation which has not yet taken place."

Carlyle was more emphatic. "Detached, separated!" he exclaimed in *Sartor Resartus*. "I say there is no such separation: nothing hitherto was ever stranded, cast aside; but all, were it only a withered leaf, works together with all; is borne forward on the bottomless, shoreless flood of Action, and lives through perpetual metamorphoses.

"Nay, if you consider it, what is Man himself, and his whole terrestrial Life, but an Emblem; a Clothing or visible Garment for that divine life of his, cast hither, like a light-particle down from Heaven?"

Robert Southey said that "the system of progressive existence seems, of all others, the most benevolent, and all that we do understand is so wise and so good, and all we do or do not, so perfectly and overwhelmingly wonderful, that the most benevolent system is the most probable."

Bulwer Lytton believed that eternity might be "an endless series of those migrations which men call deaths, abandonments of home after home, ever to fairer scenes and loftier heights. Age after age the spirit may shift its tent, fated not to rest in the dull Elysium of the heathen, but carrying with it evermore its two elements, activity and desire."

Huxley declared that none but very hasty thinkers would reject the doctrine of transmigration on the ground of inherent absurdity, since, like the doctrine of evolution, it had its roots in the world of reality, and it might claim such support as the great argument from analogy was capable of supplying.

The writings of Lafcadio Hearn contain many passages relating to Reincarnation and Karma, for he himself became a Buddhist. "For thousands of years," he wrote in *Koto*, "the East has been teaching that what we think or do in this life really decides—through some inevitable formation of atom-tendencies or polarities—the future place of our substance, and the future state of our sentiency. . . . Acts and thoughts, according to Buddhist doctrines, are creative. . . . What we think or do is never for the moment only, but for measureless time; it signifies some force directed to the shaping of worlds—to the making of future bliss or pain."

Turning to the English poets of the same period, Wordsworth seems to suggest a belief in Reincarnation in his lines:

Our birth is but a sleep and a forgetting.
The soul that rises with us, our life's star,
Hath had elsewhere its setting,
And cometh from afar,

although they promise no future incarnations. Coleridge expressed something of the same idea in the sonnet he composed "On a Journey Homeward, after hearing of the Birth of his Son, September, 1796":

Oft o'er my brain does that strange fancy roll
Which makes the present (while the flash doth
    last)
Seem a mere semblence of some unknown past,
Mix'd with such feelings as perplex the soul
Self-question'd in her sleep: and some have said
We liv'd ere yet this fleshy robe we wore.
O my sweet Baby! when I reach my door,
If heavy looks should tell me thou wert dead
(As sometimes, thro' excess of hope, I fear)
I think that I should struggle to believe
Thou wert a Spirit to this nether sphere
Sentenc'd for some more venial crime to grieve;
Didst scream, then spring to meet Heaven's quick
    reprieve,
While we wept idly o'er thy little bier.

In "Lalla Rookh" Thomas Moore likened the spirit passing from body to body to a lighted brand passed from hand to hand in a torch race, until it reaches its goal.

It seems likely that Shelley believed in Reincarnation, for Dowden has recorded that he held all knowledge to be reminiscence, and pointed out that the doctrine was far more ancient than Plato and as old as the venerable allegory that the Muses were the daughters of Memory and that none of them was ever said to be the child of invention; and in "Ariel to Miranda" his belief is suggested:

When you live again on earth,
Like an unseen star of birth
Ariel guides you o'er the sea
Of life from your nativity.
Many changes have been run
Since Ferdinand and you begun
Your course of love, and Ariel still
Has tracked your steps and served your will.

This poem shows Dante Gabriel Rossetti's belief:

I have been here before,
But when or how I cannot tell;

I know the grass beyond the door,
  The sweet keen smell,
The sighing sound, the lights around the shore

You have been mine before—
  How long ago I may not know;
But just when at the swallow's soar
  Your neck turned so,
Some veil did fall,—I knew it all of yore.

Tennyson, orthodox in most things, at least toyed with the idea in more than one of his poems:

Although I knew not in what time or place
Methought that I had often met with you,
And each had lived in other's mind and speech.

There is the same suggestion in "In Memoriam," when he reveals a "spectral doubt" that he may be Hallam's mate no more and "thro' all the secular to-be" left evermore a life behind; but in "One Word More" Browning magnificently proclaims his desire to give his all to his beloved, in this and lives to come:

I shall never, in the years remaining,
Paint you pictures, no, nor carve you statues,
Make you music that should all-express me;
So it seems: I stand on my attainment.
This of verse alone, one life allows me;
Verse and nothing else have I to give you.
Other heights in other lives, God willing:
All the gifts from all the heights, your own, Love!

Again in "Evelyn Hope" he finds consolation in
the thought that he must live again:

Is it too late then, Evelyn Hope?
*   What, your soul was pure and true,*
The good stars met in your horoscope,
*   Made you of spirit, fire and dew—*
And just because I was thrice as old,
*   And our paths in the world diverged so wide,*
Each was nought to each, must I be told?
*   We were fellow-mortals, nought beside?*

No indeed! for God above
*   Is great to grant, as mighty to make,*
And creates the love to reward the love:
*   I claim you still, for my own love's sake!*

214

Delayed it may be for more lives yet,
   Through worlds I shall traverse not a few:
Much is to learn and much to forget
   Ere the time be come for taking you.

But the time will come—at last it will,
   When, Evelyn Hope, what meant (I shall say)
In the lower earth, in the years long still,
   That body and soul so pure and gay?
Why your hair was amber, I shall divine,
   And your mouth of your own geranium's red—
And what you would do with me, in fine,
   In the new life come in the old one's stead.

In "Empedocles on Etna" Matthew Arnold showed his realization of Reincarnation's implication: and made Empedocles face them without enthusiasm:

And then we shall unwillingly return
Back to this meadow of calamity,
This uncongenial place, this human life:
And in our individual human state
Go through the sad probation all again,
To see if we will poise our life at last,

To see if we will now at last be true
To our own only true deep-buried selves,
Being one with which we are one with the whole
    world;
Or whether we will once more fall away
Into some bondage of the flesh or mind,
Some slough of sense, or some fantastic maze
Forg'd by the imperious lonely Thinking-Power.

Among the moderns, Rudyard Kipling suggested the idea of Reincarnation both in verse and prose. In "The Sack of the Gods" he expressed the sense of "Are ye not worth many sparrows" in the lines:

They will come back, come back again, as long
    as the red earth rolls.
He never wasted a leaf or tree. Do you think He
    would squander souls?

In "The Finest Story in the World" he tells how "the Fates that are so careful to shut the doors of each successive life behind us," had, in the case of Charlie Mears, the bank clerk, been neglectful, so that Charlie was able to look, though he did not know it, "where man had never been permitted to look with full knowledge since Time began," and to remember past lives as a galley slave in ancient Greece and Scandinavia.

Edward Carpenter wrote much, and beautifully, about Reincarnation, and this passage from *The Art of Creation* expresses what many must have felt:

"Here in this perennial, immeasurable consciousness sleeping within us we come again to our Celestial City, our Home from which as individuals we proceed, but from which we are never really separated. . . . Every man feels doubtless that his little mortal life is very inadequate, and that to express and give utterance to all that is in him would need many lives, many bodies. Even what we have been able to say here shows that the deeper self of him—that which is the source of all his joy and inspiration—has had the experience of many lives, many bodies, and will have."

"A.E.," in a lovely poem, imagines himself walking the ways of ancient Babylon, with the voice he loves whispering in his ear:

Oh real as in dream all this; and then a hand on
*   mine is laid:*
The wave of phantom time withdraws; and that
*   young Babylonian maid,*
One drop of beauty left behind from all the
*   flowing of that tide,*
Is looking with the self-same eyes, and here in
*   Ireland by my side.*
Oh light our life in Babylon, but Babylon has
*   taken wings,*
While we are in the calm and proud procession of
*   eternal things.*

Clifford Bax, commenting on those lines in "Inland Far" said that when he read them he might still have adduced objection to the theory of Reincarnation, but something within him had apprehended that it was true.

"A man became for me now the protagonist of a stupendous saga," he wrote. "Behind him I saw innumerable lives that stretched far back beyond even the first ages of the earth, an endless record of slow descent into matter, a chain of cause and effect that had its origin only in the Darkness

Thrice Unknown from which the whole universe
had once been emanated: and before him I saw
the unborn aeons through which he should travel
on the 'homeward way'; life after life rising like a
vision of mountain-peaks beheld from the top of
the Apennines, and fading into the dim bloom of
a distance immeasurably withdrawn, until at last,
transformed from a filth-eating fool to a spirit of
unimaginable beauty, he should put on the gnos-
tic 'Robe of Glory' and be lost in the central light."

A passage from Algernon Blackwood's *Episodes before Thirty* is worth quoting for its com-
prehension of the problem of the unequalness in
the "soul ages" of people gathered together in
contemporary life:

" 'Old Souls' and 'Young Souls' was a classifi-
cation that ruled my mind in this period. . . . In
the Old lay innate the fruits, the results, the
memories of many, many previous lives, and the
ripeness of long experience showed itself in certain ways—in taste, in judgment, in their standard
of values, in that mysterious quality called tact:
above all, perhaps, in the type and quality of

goods they desired from life. Worldly ambitions, so-called, were generally negligible in them. What we label to-day as the subconscious was invariably fully charged; also, without too much difficulty, accessible. It made them interesting, stimulating, not easily exhausted. Wide sympathies, spread charity, and understanding were their hallmarks, and a certain wisdom, as apart from intellect, their invariable gift; with, moreover, a tendency to wit, if not that rare quality wit itself, and humour, the power of seeing, and therefore laughing at, oneself. The cheaper experiences of birth, success, possessions, they had learned long ago; it was the more difficult, but higher values they had come back to master, and among the humbler ranks of life they found the necessary conditions. Christ, I reflected, was the son of a carpenter. The Young Souls, on the other hand, were invariably hot-foot after the things of this world—Show, Riches, and Power stuck like red labels on their foreheads. The Napoleons of the earth were among the youngest of all; the intellectuals, those who relied on reason alone, often the prosperous, usually the well-born, were of the same category. Rarely was 'understanding' in them; a brilliant cleverness could never rank with that wisdom which knows that *tout comprendre c'est tout pardonner.* To me the Young Souls were the commonplace and uninteresting ones. They were shallow, sketchy, soon exhausted, the *Dutzendmenschen*: whereas the others were intuitive, mature in outlook, aware of deeper values and eager for the things of the spirit."

There is nothing to show that Mr Bernard Shaw believes in Reincarnation, but in *Back to Methuselah* he stated the case perfectly in a dialogue between Savvy and Conrad. In reply to Savvy, who suspects she is Eve ("I am very fond of apples; and they always disagree with me"), Conrad says:

"You *are* Eve in a sense. The Eternal Life persists; only It wears out Its bodies and minds and gets new ones, like new clothes. You are only a new hat and frock on Eve."

In *Later Days* W. H. Davies recognized the

working of the Law of Karma, if he did not fully understand that to every man is given the freedom to forbear:

"I still have my own ideas of a future state. It is this—that if we are hunted and pursued in this life by malicious enemies, so, in the life to come, it is we that will be the hunters and our enemies the hunted. This idea comes from no vindictive spirit. . . . It comes from the knowledge that I have never wilfully done harm to anyone on earth. My capacity for taking punishment has been tremendous, but the spirit to inflict it on another was not given to me at birth. But in this new life to come, it will be the decree of the reigning powers that I shall ride on the backs of my enemies, and they will live in fear of me from hour to hour."

But to me the finest exposition of Reincarnation ever put into words by a poet are John Masefield's seven stanzas, of which these are the first and last:

I hold that when a person dies
  His soul returns again to earth;

Arrayed in some new flesh-disguise,
*   Another mother gives him birth.*
With sturdier limbs and brighter brain
The old soul takes the road again. . . .

So shall I fight, so shall I tread,
*   In this long war beneath the stars;*
So shall a glory wreathe my head,
*   So shall I faint and show the scars,*
Until this case, this clogging mould,
Be smithied all to kingly gold.

TEN

How Debts Are Adjusted

No one is likely to accept a philosophy which does not appeal to him, nor is he necessarily to be convinced of its truth because, throughout the ages, men of intelligence have accepted it. Nevertheless, although few people are influenced by argument, many are glad to listen to explanation; and in the explanation of other people's sufferings they may be able to find the cause of much that has bewildered them in their own lives.

Let us first consider collective suffering, such as that involved by an earthquake. Here, apparently, Nature is striking, not man claiming the adjustment of an old debt. Why, it may be asked, should thousands be killed in this way, or made homeless? Why should such suffering be meted out to women and young children?

First of all, I think we should disabuse ourselves of the idea that women, by mere virtue of their sex, are entitled to be treated more leniently than men. Karma postulates justice, and it would be palpably unjust if women were not required to bear the same responsibility for their acts as men. Indeed, they may have been men when they committed those acts, although even so they would not be given more than they could bear in women's bodies. So with children: no child can suffer for what it has not earned; and children mercifully suffer less and succumb quicker than older people. But if a man tortures a child, he must eventually be placed in the position of experiencing similar torture in a child's body. In Lawrence's *Seven Pillars of Wisdom* there are some terrible stories of the manner in which the Turks spitted babies upon their bayonets. Each one would have to make due restitution to the child, and to suffer as a child as well.

We must suppose, therefore, that those who perish in an earthquake or similar disaster were due to acquire just that experience and were gathered together to make adjustment at the same time. Is it difficult to believe that each one of those who suffered had, at one time or another, turned his back on one who had sought his aid, or refused to help the homeless, even if he had not himself caused the loss of home or inflicted physical or mental torture? Nor must we forget that a great national disaster, besides bringing ruin and distress, gives those who are involved in it many opportunities of working off karma by helping the afflicted, and of strengthening character by displaying courage in adversity. Those who understand should welcome the chances given, rather than bewail the sufferings of others.

Let us take another aspect of collective suffering. To Hitler, better than to any other man alive, could be applied the saying "It must needs be that offences come; but woe unto that man by whom the offence cometh." Hitler's career is an excellent example of the individual's freedom of choice. After he had secured power in Germany, he was presented with one of the greatest opportunities a political leader has ever had in history. The German people were distressed and disillusioned. He had the chance of giving them fresh hope, of leading them back to prosperity. To some extent he did so, and served his country for good, just as Mussolini had served Italy. Like Mussolini, Hitler restored courage and self-confidence to the youth of his nation and gave it an incentive for living; and this is one of the greatest, if not the greatest, service a leader can render his fellow men and women.

Hitler's personal tragedy is not the evil in his character, but the good. Past experience appears to have given him nearly all the attributes of a great leader: the desire to serve, singleness of aim, integrity of purpose, simplicity of life, and that sublime resolution which sweeps obstacles from its path and awakens response in others. All this experience Hitler gathered in one life or another, how we cannot tell, and returned to earth with it in his present incarnation, when it was put to the test. But the one thing he had not learned in the past was to use his experience well: that is to say, he is a "young soul," in that he has not yet learned tolerance and balance, the fruits of wisdom. Hitler's balance is that of the spinning top, whipped to momentum from without, rather than the sustained poise which is the outcome of long training.

The result has been that such wisdom as he had became obscured by the thirst for power. He grew like a spendthrift who succeeds to riches. His inheritance brought out the worst in him rather than the best, and the very position his good qualities had won for him became a test of his bad ones. In that test he failed. Leaving the middle way he abandoned himself to extremes: the ideal of service changed to compulsion, enthusiasm bred fanaticism, resolution bred intolerance and cruelty, and personal integrity was subordinated to the obsessing aim of domination. But even with this he could not be content. And as time passed he became not only the immediate cause of suffering to others by his personal commands, but the indirect cause of even greater suffering by his system and through his followers, many of whom excelled him in fanaticism.

The time comes when such a man must make reparation to thousands. It may be that when Hitler's time comes he will reappear in incarnation as a great social reformer. He will then have all the good qualities which he brought to his present incarnation, and, for his sake it may be hoped, by that time may have learned to use them more wisely. Thus he may be enabled to work off in a single life much of the bad karma he has made necessary by his actions in this one.

History shows that whenever civilization has produced great abuses, a reformer arises to put an end to them. Such a man, I feel sure, has learned humanitarianism from past mistakes. Men like Lord Shaftesbury, who devoted his life to improving the conditions of factory workers,

and particularly of the child-workers, and Wilber-
force, who was instrumental in abolishing slavery,
may once have been great industrialists or slave-
owners in Egypt or Rome. Dim memory of past
suffering may have encouraged them to do this
work, and thereby to pay off karma collectively,
their memories having been stimulated, perhaps,
by having in an earlier life made partial adjustment in experiencing what it meant to be a slave.

Another such reformer was Samuel Plimsoll
who, after a long struggle against the opposition of
vested interests, succeeded in improving the conditions of merchant seamen. His reforms saved the
lives of thousands, and it may well be that he himself in an earlier existence had been a shipowner
who had sent ill-found and ill-conditioned "coffin
ships" to sea, indifferent to the lives of those who
manned them. The shipowners who opposed him,
men who made great fortunes if the ships reached
port and collected heavy insurance if they did not,
one would expect to find in a shipping disaster
such as that of the *Titanic* or the *Lusitania*, until at

last they learned the lesson which Plimsoll had learned before them.

Sir Humphrey Davy is another example. He may have been a mine-owner who had worked his people beyond endurance and, having learned wisdom, returned to help his fellows by the invention of his safety lamp. Men such as these, sowing, as it seems, anonymous benefits upon the world by their reforms and their inventions, are in reality seizing the chances offered them to pay off karma on a large scale.

A person who had helped another in the accumulation of wealth, or shown charity when he was in poor circumstances, might himself become entitled to handle wealth in his next life, being born, perhaps, as the heir to a rich father. This is one of the severest tests of character: but he would have free will to act. He might use his wealth wisely and with compassion, trying to benefit the lot of his less fortunate fellow creatures. Or he might mishandle it, and squander it. One would expect to find a man who failed to accept his responsibilities reincarnating in a slum, hankering for riches, or as a Communist barking at the capitalist system.

Cases of blindness might be explained in more than one way. It might be that the blind person had himself wilfully deprived another of his sight; or he might have been an employer who worked his people in a factory until they went blind. Such a person might return to earth with a dim memory of the wrongs he had inflicted upon others and then might be expected to devote himself to the cause of the blind. One such case has come to my notice. A man who had worked unceasingly for many years in the cause of the blind, himself lost his sight; but it so happened that he was led to a surgeon who offered to perform a difficult operation, which proved entirely successful. Here one can see memory causing the man to make reparation, and karma working out, but alleviated because his compassion had earned him the right to have his blindness removed.

So with the deaf and dumb. In olden days the piercing of ears and the slitting of tongues was no uncommon form of torture. Or it might be that the present sufferer had abused his faculties by listening at doors to secrets, or by slandering his fellows. In such a case a man would have to learn what it feels like to be slandered: and here may be an explanation of those "poison pen" campaigns, when apparently perfectly innocent people are made to suffer and forced to leave their homes. So, too, with blackmail, one of the most terrible forms of mental torture: the victim must himself have victimized the blackmailer in the past.

A man has a duty to care for his own body, and one would expect to find those who have neglected to do so ailing in this life, in weak bodies which need continual tending, while the athletes and the robust are those who have looked after their bodies in the past and so have become entitled to strong physical constitutions.

The case of a childless couple, who ardently desire to have children, is not uncommon, and can be explained, perhaps, on the ground that in a previous life they have declined to have children when they had the opportunity. For a woman there is no sadder form of frustrated longing; but Reincarnation gives her the promise that she will attain the fulfilment of her hopes once the mistakes of the past have been adjusted: a hope she could not have if life on earth were restricted to one existence.

Arrogance and self-sufficiency would make it necessary for a man to return in a weak body, and to live under severe discipline; cruelty, whether physical or mental, would entail pain and persecution in the next life. Or it might be that a man would be shown the error of his behaviour away from earth. There is a case on record of a foxhunter who dreamed of being hunted as a fox and abandoned hunting from that day.

Humility is one of the most difficult, and one of the most frequent, lessons man has to learn, and pride, particularly intellectual pride, must entail being reborn in humble circumstances, and having to serve under a mental inferior.

As I have suggested, success in the arts or in a profession must be the result of constant striving and training in previous lives; but that training may have been developed to the exclusion of other necessary experience. The specialist may be brilliant at his own work but ignorant and incompetent in other lines of training. A specialist was once defined as one who knows more and more about less and less, and such a man would have to return to learn other lessons which he had neglected.

This would apply even more to the genius, who, as history shows, is only too often intolerant of others and may inflict mental torture on those about him. Having reached the peak of his special training, it might be necessary for his talent to be obscured when he returned to earth. His memory would then still be active, but his capacity of performance limited, and thus he might learn his lesson through being unable to do what he most yearned to do, since his memory would give him instinctive taste, while the gift of creation was withheld until he had put right the harm his selfishness had caused. The highly developed training, however, although temporarily obscured, would not be obliterated.

Many burglars are connoisseurs of the fine arts, memory, no doubt, of taste acquired in surroundings happier than their present ones. Moreover, the practice of burgling tends to develop patience, courage, skill, and organizing ability. When a burglar has paid off the karma he has incurred for stealing, he would still have these qualities to his credit, since no experience gained is ever lost.

It is worth examining the possible karma of a burglar who forcibly enters a house and steals a quantity of jewelry. He is then due to make amends for breaking the law of the land, and he must, sooner or later, also make restitution to the person whose goods he has stolen. It may be that he is arrested, convicted and sent to prison for seven years. In this way he puts himself right with the law and the experience gained may teach him to be a better citizen: in his next incarnation his conscience would be reinforced by the knowledge that it was not worth while to steal. There remains the personal debt. Possibly the jewelry was insured and paid for, so that the owner would suffer little more than inconvenience, and there can scarcely be a direct karmic liability to an insurance company. But it might be that among the articles stolen, and not recovered, was some trifle of no intrinsic value but of great sentimental interest to the possessor. Then, one may believe, it might take a long time to pay off that debt, for the thief would have to make good the mental suffering incurred. It might be many lives before he was placed in the position of making adequate restitution—by performing the loser a service when he was in dire distress—even though the value of the gift might be but trifling. Such a debt cannot be reckoned in material terms, since it would be the mental disturbance, rather than the pecuniary loss, which would demand adjustment.

It is, of course, difficult, indeed impossible, to know whether the individual whose goods are stolen, or who is cheated by an impostor, is not himself paying an old debt. A personal incident will furnish an example. Not long ago a young man appeared at my front door and asked me for help. He was well dressed and well spoken, with neatly brushed sandy hair and frank blue eyes.

He told his tale with disarming candour and much circumstantial detail. He had been a student at McGill University in Canada, he said, and had lately returned to his home in Folkestone to find that his father had married again. He had resented a newcomer in his mother's place, and when his father insisted that he should call her "mother" he had refused. Thereupon his father had turned him out of the house without a penny. So he had set out to walk to Chester, where he had an uncle who would look after him.

"All I want is to get to Chester, sir," he said, looking straight into my eyes. "Will you lend me a pound to help me on my way? Will you give me a break? Will you trust me? I promise I'll send you the money back in three days. Once I get to my uncle, I'll be all right."

I had no means of knowing whether he was telling me the truth. I had, indeed, no reason to disbelieve him. I felt that if I disbelieved him, and his story were genuine, I should be doing him a wrong. I might, of course, have rung up the police and asked them to make inquiries. I might have demanded his uncle's address and sent a telegram to verify his story. But I liked the boy, and I felt I could trust him. I handed him over a pound note.

Before he went, I said:

"I'm prepared to believe your story. But if it's not true, I advise you not to take the money, because it isn't likely to do you any good."

At that he looked at me with his frank smile.

"On my word of honour, sir," he said.

I never heard of him again.

I consoled myself with the thought that, cheat or no cheat, he probably needed the pound more than I, and I felt it not unlikely that I had been given the opportunity of paying off an old debt. If not, I knew the time would come when he would have to offer to pay me back. It may be that I should have refused to help him, or made inquiries, to prevent others from being victimized. As it was, when I found that he had tricked me I felt rather sorry for him. He was a nice boy and I have no doubt that, even though an old debt between us was settled, he will, sooner or later, have to suffer the experience of being cheated in a similar way, since within his memory is the consciousness of successful deception; and that, most certainly, will have to be erased.

The causes which set up certain aspects of Karma, as suggested in this chapter, cannot be proved by the rules of evidence and must remain a matter of speculation. The cause is less important than the lesson to be learned from the effect; and we need not doubt that our past conduct, even if we cannot determine it with exactitude, has made it necessary that we should learn. He who is prepared to accept his lesson will save himself frustration and unhappiness. But that acceptance must come from within. It must be more than objective acknowledgment or a mere profession of fault. It is not enough to recognize one's failings: recognition, certainly, is something, but of no value unless correction follows, for the lesson will be repeated until it has become accepted as an integral part of his conscience and so enriched his experience.

ELEVEN

Practical Application

Some people are accustomed to look upon their religion as a best suit. But one cannot be religious on Sundays and pagan the rest of the week. If religion remains objective it can be of little more practical help in life than a knowledge of Homeric Greek. A man's faith should be a living language not a dead one. It should also be a staff rather than an umbrella, a support rather than a shield. It must have a practical application to every phase of life. Love, the poet tells us, is in man's life a thing apart, 'tis woman's whole existence. Faith, like love, is nothing if it is a thing apart; it must pervade our lives—*be* our lives.

It is essential, therefore, that there should be no mystery about it, for how can men and women put into practice what they do not understand? As I have tried to show, the essence of the teaching of all the Great Masters was its simplicity. Their followers, and those who came after them, elaborated the original teaching, embroidering it with ritual and dogma. But the light inside a bulb is not less bright because the glass is painted blue: we do but see the light obscured. And, as I have also tried to show, the old teaching still shines brightly for those who have eyes to see and speaks clearly for those who have ears to hear. It is simple, it is logical, it is practical. But if, knowing it, we do not put our knowledge into practice, but merely accept it intellectually, we are no better off than those who accept worn out dogma without question, or order their lives on the predictions of diviners.

"If we are the slaves of the past, if fate compels us to reap what we have sown, we yet have the future in our hands," wrote Théophile Pascal, "for we can tear up the weeds, and in their place sow useful plants. Just as, by means of physical hygiene, we can change within a few years the nature of the constituents that make up our bodies, so also, by a process of moral hygiene, we can purify our passions and then turn their strength in the direction of good."

The Law of Karma cannot be kept apart from human life, because it is the process by which life progresses: simply cause and effect translated into terms of individual behaviour. We can see Karma working out all round us, every minute of the day, in our own lives and in the lives of our friends.

As I have shown, every action done produces a corresponding result, good or bad, which affects not only the doer but more usually, one or more other people. That is to say, if Jones does Brown an injury, both are affected in different ways. Jones must, sooner or later, make the necessary adjustment. Brown will be given the opportunity to exact payment, but he may exact that payment only to the extent of the injury he received, and no more; if, in the heat of revenge, he exacts more than that to which he is entitled, he himself incurs a corresponding debt to Jones. Thus the situation is a test not only for Jones but also for Brown, and all the more so because, although Brown is entitled to demand quittance, he is not *required* to do so. He may show forbearance to Jones by declining to exact restitution; by doing so he will dissipate an old debt and at the same time extend his quality of mercy.

This opportunity to show forbearance is always present, and is a most important part of the Law. The uninformed sometimes contend that Karma is vengeance. It is the reverse, since a man has free choice to take revenge or to show mercy. Jesus said, "Ye have heard that it hath been said, An eye for an eye, and a tooth for a tooth: But I say unto you, That ye resist not evil: but whosoever shall smite thee on thy right cheek, turn to him the other also." (*Matthew, v,* 38, 39). This has been the teaching of every Great Master.

If Brown remits the debt, adjustment between him and Jones is made, but that does not absolve Jones from having to learn his lesson. If he has been cruel to Brown, Brown may forbear to make himself an instrument of Karma, but Jones will still have to learn what cruelty is, although by his own behaviour he may lessen, or even obviate, the karma due.

This theme is the fountain of all dramatic literature. Shakespeare's tragedies abound in examples of the working out of karma, and none better than "The Merchant of Venice."

Antonio borrowed 3,000 ducats from Shylock not on his own behalf, but to oblige his friend Bassanio. Now it is perfectly clear that Antonio had no more love for Jews than a Nazi has to-day. He had told Shylock, who was in fact one of the most prominent merchants in Venice, that he was

> *Like a villain with a smiling cheek;*
> *A goodly apple with a rotten core,*

and had even gone so far as to call him "misbeliever, cut-throat dog." Thus Antonio, by his arrogance, owed Shylock a debt of manners before he even incurred a debt of money, and sooner or later Shylock would be placed in a position to exact payment of his injury. When Antonio needed money, Shylock lent it, and insisted upon the preposterous bond in the hope that Antonio would fail to repay the loan, so that he could then exact requital for his humiliation. His chance came when Antonio's ships went astray. In spite of Antonio's plea, he refused 6,000 ducats, intent on the pound of flesh.

> *I'll have my bond; speak not against my bond:*
> *I have sworn an oath that I will have my bond.*
> *Thou call'st me dog before thou had'st a cause;*
> *But since I am a dog, beware my fangs.*

When Portia came to examine the bond she admitted that

> *Lawfully by this the Jew may claim*
> *A pound of flesh, to be by him cut off*
> *Nearest the merchant's heart,*

but when Shylock had whetted his knife she warned him that:

The bond doth give thee here no jot of blood;
The words expressly are "a pound of flesh":
Then take thy bond, and take thy pound of flesh;
But in the cutting of it, if thou dost shed
One drop of Christian blood, thy lands and goods
Are, by the laws of Venice, confiscate.

Here, then, is an excellent example of the creditor not being allowed to take more than his exact due. In attempting to collect more than that, Shylock himself incurred bad karma: his wealth was forfeit because he, as an alien, had sought to take the life of a Venetian citizen. Here Antonio earned merit for forbearance. He did not exact payment, and by his humiliation at Shylock's hands he paid for his arrogance. The debt between them was adjusted, but not the enmity. If the characters had existed in real life the feud might have persisted for many lives to come, Antonio baiting Shylock in one life, Shylock oppressing Antonio in the next. Antonio might have been reborn a Jew in Fascist Italy or in Nazi Germany so that he could experience what Jew-baiting meant, while Shylock might have been placed in a position to learn the use or abuse of power. As a Fascist leader, Shylock might use his authority rightly and forbear to persecute Antonio when he had the opportunity, having learned that lesson in the meantime, or, not having learned it, he might take advantage of his position and cause Antonio to be driven from his country as a refugee. Then Shylock would again become the persecuted in his turn, until the old enmity between him and Antonio became finally adjusted and they could meet as friends.

The story of Macbeth is another dramatic example of Karma working out. Here we may suppose that Macbeth was placed in a position of power to learn the dangers of overweening ambition. In the sum his character was noble. He was a great warrior, loyal to his king until the test, with a streak of weakness which he had not yet learnt to overcome. In Shakespeare's version of the tragedy he is seen grappling with his conscience and refusing to heed the warning against the murder of the king.

How oft the sight of means to do ill deeds
Makes ill deeds done—

but the doer has free will to do them or to refrain.

Karma does but set the situation, and man may either emerge triumphant or fail. Macbeth failed. He made requital in the same incarnation by the downfall of his hopes, so that, when faced in a later incarnation with a similar situation, he would have the memory of the experience to help him to act rightly, but the adjustment with Duncan and Banquo was left until later. Whether each exacted his due when given the opportunity, we cannot tell.

Karma need not necessarily be delayed until another incarnation; often, as I have shown, we pay as we go. We should not be loth to accept service from others, voluntarily offered, in the fear of incurring debts which must be paid off, for it may well be that the opportunities to do just these services are to enable our friends to adjust debts due to us. And if we understand the Law and practise it, we should be thankful—or at least philosophical—when disagreeable things come to us, knowing that here is an opportunity to work off karma which must be paid sooner or later. Admittedly this needs the highest degree of wisdom, patience and courage, but thought will show that any other attitude to misfortune must be inconsistent, and we may rest assured in the knowledge that we shall be protected from all ill that's not due to us.

Illness, like the other misfortunes to which human life is subject, is karmic and is to be explained only on the grounds that the sufferer has made it necessary. Severe pain may be the result of cruelty in another life, which has made it necessary for a person to experience what he himself inflicted. Or again it may be the result of the abuse of the body in the past. Some illness is not intended to be cured in one life; otherwise, when the sufferer has earned the right to be healed, a healer will be brought across his path.

Now I fully realize that it is one thing for a person physically fit to accept intellectually the theory that illness is but the result of his own previous acts, and quite another for a person who is actually in acute physical pain. For instance, it is not easy for a person suffering from arthritis to believe that his condition is due to suffering he caused another in a previous life. At first thought it will certainly bring him no comfort; it may indeed arouse his indignation. But once the mental adjustment has been made, it will at least remove the feeling of injustice which every suffering person must feel from time to time. Why should I have to suffer like this when my friends, who are no better than I, are fit and well? Thoughts such as this must come to everyone.

Once a sufferer realizes the reason of his pain, this feeling of injustice and resentment must vanish, and thereby a certain amount of mental anguish is removed; understanding that the effect has been induced only by the cause, even though the actual details of the cause remain unknown, the patient is on the road to learn the lesson which the pain was sent to teach him. It will also, I believe, give him courage to strive with his unhappy condition, rather than to give way to it and submit; and every doctor knows that a patient's own attitude to his health materially aids or retards his recovery.

The very effort made to throw off the illness may be what is necessary for the suffering to be removed. Nothing but the Law of Karma can explain the apparent inconsistency of the course of illness. When, for example, two patients are suffering from the same complaint, the treatment which cures one will have no visible effect upon the other, the explanation being that the first patient has made his adjustment, and so has earned the right to be cured, while the other has still more to learn.

If acceptance of the Law of Karma helps men and women to understand the necessity of illness, it will also help them to understand war, which is but another malady made necessary by mankind. Wars have been since the beginning of earth and it is probable that there will continue to be wars until the spiritual evolution of this planet is complete.

If a number of children are left together in a

nursery, it will not be long before one or other of them tries to snatch his companions' toys. Little Johnny, who has been given a perfectly good box of bricks to play with, gets tired of building houses and begins to look with envy on the clock-work engine to which Richard is devoting his attention. He leaves his bricks and watches Richard. "I want it," he announces, stretching forth an acquisitive hand. Richard demurs. Johnny lays hands upon the engine. Richard clutches it tighter to his chest with both hands. A struggle ensues, in which Johnny, if he be the stronger, emerges triumphant, leaving Richard, bereft of his engine, to howl, or, if he has the makings of a warrior, to fight for his own.

This process, commonly called the give and take of the nursery, is to be seen at work in the larger world of international politics. Most wars are due, not to nations, but to the acquisitiveness of an individual who is in a position of power and encourages others to follow him. The saying of Jesus, "He who lives by the sword shall perish with the sword," is a warning that he who makes war

THE SCALES OF KARMA

without a just cause must make adjustment: and here, as always, it is the motive which counts.

It must needs be that offences must come: that is to say, war is part of the Plan by which evolution is to be worked out, but the individuals in power are free to make war or to refrain from making it. I believe that, once a country has become involved in war, its male citizens of fighting age do their duty by joining the army, and I am convinced that they will incur no bad karma for killing their country's enemies in the course of their duties as soldiers, unless they glory in the killing. That is to say, a citizen is justified in fighting for his country, so long as he obeys the laws and usages of war, and fights cleanly and chivalrously as a brave warrior, showing mercy to the fallen and respect to the vanquished.

There is a difference between fighting with determination and fighting with hate. In the war of 1914–18 no troops displayed greater resolution than the British private soldiers, but it was impossible for them to work up a hate against the enemy. I well remember my commanding officer once exclaiming, "You Wiltshiremen, you're too damned goodnatured!" after it had been impressed upon him by G.H.Q. that we must show more "offensive spirit." It was not that they were half-hearted about fighting, but they could not feel any personal antagonism for the enemy. And a prisoner had not been in our hands five minutes before he was loaded with cigarettes and chocolate in return for the buttons from his tunic, to be carefully preserved as "souvenirs."

That is the way in which war should be fought, and that is how war, with all its horror and pain and suffering, can bring out the better and higher qualities in those who have to engage in it, just as it may bring out cruelty and lust for blood, and perhaps cowardice. Nor was the spirit of chivalry confined in the last war to the British troops and their allies. Our erstwhile enemies the Turks always fought like gentlemen, and so did many of the Germans, particularly the airmen and some of the sailors, such as the captain of the raider *Emden*.

The object of war is to destroy the enemy's

effective striking power, in accordance with agreed conventions, which have now become one-sided. Operations with that object in view are legitimate; those which contravene the conventions of war are not. A prisoner taken is as effective as a man killed; therefore mercy must be shown, and I would not care to have the karma of one who kills a soldier who has surrendered, or runs his bayonet through a wounded man. I should imagine that the karma of an armaments manufacturer who deliberately stirred up war so that he might profit from it, would be the least enviable of all.

In the present war we have already seen the difference between the cruel and the chivalrous warrior in the submarine commanders who torpedo merchant ships without warning, thereby causing death and suffering to non-combatants, and so incurring terrible karma for themselves, and those who pay heed to international law by giving due warning and by caring for the crews of the vessels they destroy.

For the fighting man, war offers great and immediate opportunities of working off karma and for gaining experience by the courage, service, patience and endurance which war entails. But it does far more than that. In earlier days, almost up to the twentieth century, war had little effect upon the civilian population, at all events in England, which never suffered from invasion. Non-combatants went about their lives much as usual, and only those whose husbands, or sons, or brothers, were fighting had cause for personal anxiety. Jane Austen's novels were set during the period of the Napoleonic wars: but there is scarcely a mention of war in them. Certainly the Miss Bennetts made no attempt to serve in canteens or to work in hospitals.

In modern warfare conditions are entirely different, and affect the whole civilian population, women as much as men. Women played a great and valiant part in the war of 1914–18. To-day they play an even more important part, and the threat of air attack affects even the lives of children. The evacuation of cities has given hundreds of thousands of women and children the opportunity of working off karma by facing discomforts and changed conditions with cheerfulness and courage, to a degree previously inconceivable in this country. Women who had never done a day's work in their lives now drive lorries or become V.A.D.s, or work long hours in canteens. War is giving them innumerable chances of serving not only their country but also their fellow human beings in a way they would not have thought possible before.

Nobody dislikes war more than I do, but that does not prevent me from seeing to-day—as I could not see during the last war—that, once begun, it has its purpose. I used to find it difficult to understand how, if there were a benevolent deity, he could allow wholesale butchery to take place. Now, although not without difficulty, I have come to accept the fact that in a hundred ways war assists and speeds up evolution by giving opportunity for karma to be worked off in a short space: the periods of greatest difficulty are the times of greatest advancement.

I do not pretend that such an attitude makes war any more agreeable, but it does make it more intelligible, and that means a great deal. On every hand I see willing and devoted service being given by those who fight, by those who remain at home, by those who have to wait with anxious hearts for news of loved ones on active service: the hardest test of all. Courage and loyalty, patience and sympathy, friendliness and unselfish devotion—all these qualities war evokes; and they are not little things.

Thus thousands upon thousands benefit by such experience. Those whose earth bodies are due to be killed, will die, whether they are in the front line, in a bombing plane, in ships at sea, in a cellar during an air raid, in an accident during the black-out, or in one of those "safe areas" advertised by people who want to let their houses.

Although it is right to take reasonable precaution for one's safety, a sense of proportion is necessary in this, as in all other matters; and it seems to me that A.R.P. has caused many people to become too preoccupied with the problem of personal safety. I did not care for what I saw during the crisis in September, 1938, when thousands of business men bolted from London and tried to buy houses in the West of England and elsewhere. Much of what I have seen since the outbreak of the present war I like still less. It is not good, surely, for a nation which is waging what has proved to be the most bitter war in history to act upon the principle of "safety first." London, with every building displaying arrows to air raid shelters, breeds a spirit of apprehension which Londoners never knew in the last war. "Safety Amidst Charming Surroundings" ran one advertisement I read: those who took advantage of it were unlikely to gain the experience which modern war offers everyone, nor was the woman who offered: "Beautifully furnished 4-room all-electric dream country cottage; no children."

I felt moved to parody the epitaph on the Spartans who fell at Thermopylae:

Tell London, ye who pass this tenement,
We ran from her, and here we rest content.

But in truth God is not mocked. "There is no armour against fate, death lays his icy hands on kings"—and those who seek safety in the moors of Devon when they might be performing useful service will not escape when their mark is reached, while, as I have suggested, Karma explains others' apparently miraculous escapes from death. In wartime it is more than ever necessary to keep before us the knowledge that only the physical body can be killed. "Be not afraid of them that kill the body, and after that have no more that they can do." (*Luke, xii,* 4).

In war, as in every other affair of daily life, he who understands something of Karma knows that the laws of the land in which he has incarnated are the best discipline for him; he will not be wrong if he follows them. But, should he believe them to be contrary to the dictates of his own conscience, his motive for breaking them, or for not following them, would be taken into account when his karma was assessed.

John Bunyan, we may be sure, earned no bad karma for giving his teaching in defiance of the law, although he had to suffer the discomfort of imprisonment; and men such as Charles Dickens who direct their efforts to securing wise changes in the law, can earn nothing but good karma. In the same way a man who honestly believed that it was wrong to fight in any circumstances would earn no bad karma. Indeed, our own law makes provision for his scruples, so long as he can prove them to be genuine. The moral courage entailed in withstanding popular opinion would help to strengthen his character, while one who tried to hide behind the "conscientious objector" provisions with the mere object of saving his own skin would find his cowardice unavailing. It seems likely that so strongly a developed disinclination to fight—for whatever reason—must be due to the memory of some terrible experience in war in a recent incarnation. Indeed, we may believe that it is only the memory of having fought and suffered in countless wars which slowly builds up a love of peace.

TWELVE

The Goal of Attainment

I believe that karma can be incurred and paid off while we are away from our earth bodies during sleep. It is necessary, therefore, to consider the nature of sleep and to understand the difference between sleep and death.

I find myself able to accept the belief, which was taught by the priests in Ancient Egypt, that every person has seven bodies. His physical composition consists of the earth body, the overcoat as it were; the etheric body, which interpenetrates the earth body and acts as its battery, receiving life; and the sub-mental body, the thought-switch which conveys ideas and intentions to the earth body. The soul is composed of the astral body, which registers our emotions, and the two mental bodies: the low mental, which we use for thinking of concrete and impermanent things, and the affairs of every day life, and the high mental, the heart of the soul, which we use for abstract thought and reflection upon permanent things. These six bodies make up the personality, which we renew in each reincarnation. The seventh body is the buddhaic body, the material for furnishing growth for the real self, the spirit, which is the granary of memory and the sum of all the experience gained in all our lives. This is the individuality, which persists like an undying flame, life after life, and is born again in a fresh physical body with a new personality. Its symbol was the lotus, which, although embodied in mud, pushes upwards towards the light.

To charge the physical battery, the etheric body, with new life, sleep is necessary, but while we are asleep we are able to continue our activities on the astral plane, making use of the astral body, which is attached to the earth body by the silver cord, composed of matter so fine that it has been described as "the ghost of a piece of cotton."

The twelfth chapter of Ecclesiastes contains a beautiful description of the death of the earth body: "Or ever the silver cord be loosed, or the golden bowl be broken, or the pitcher be broken at the fountain, or the wheel broken at the cistern." The loosing of the silver cord frees the astral body from its thraldom. The golden bowl is the submental body, which tips thought into the cistern, the earth body. The pitcher is the etheric body, which holds life as a pitcher holds water, and pours it out into the earth body. In the ancient Egyptian houses the water supply, stored in a cistern, was pumped through the pipes by a wheel. So that the breaking of the golden bowl symbolized thought no longer capable of being

expressed through the body; the breaking of the
pitcher symbolized the etheric unable to contain
force from the fountain of life; the broken wheel
symbolized the stilled movements of the body
from which cistern came neither thought nor life.

Once the silver cord has been loosed, the astral
body does not return, but remains on its own
plane. This is the only difference between sleep
and death, and I am convinced that after death we
continue to move on the astral plane as we did
when our earth bodies were alive, so long as we
have knowledge of where we are, and of what we
are about. Those who have chained themselves in
life to material things, and those who meet violent ends or die in terror, tend to become earthbound by images of their own creation. Such a
one lives in a frozen moment, able to think only
of his condition at the time of death. That is why
ghosts whose appearance is recorded are nearly
always unhappy, and here perhaps is the explanation of that ancient prayer "From battle,
murder and sudden death, good Lord deliver us."
At first thought, most people would welcome sud-

den death rather than lingering illness; but the maker of the prayer must have been well aware that the too-sudden loosing of the silver cord might leave the astral body bewildered and unprepared, with no time to commend the spirit into the hands of God.

"A good name is better than precious ointment," said the Preacher, "and the day of death than the day of one's birth." There is no cynicism in that saying, but a message of hope. The fear of death is the fear of the unknown. But those who know that, instead of returning to earth, they are to remain for a while on a familiar plane, must find happiness in the assurance that the Plan in which each has a part goes on after the loosing of the silver cord, and that they have further opportunities of gaining experience while they are resting from their sojourn upon earth and awaiting their next incarnation.

Death has a new significance if we can regard it not as the end of life but as the beginning of new experiences, and if we can look upon the waiting time before rebirth as a period of refreshment before the spirit takes up new tasks, so that each death is a stage on the way to evolution, rather than the terminus of a journey. "Each time we die," said Victor Hugo, "we gain more of life."

Samuel Butler regarded death as the dissolving of a partnership, the partners to which survive and go elsewhere. "It is the corruption or breaking up of that society which we have called Ourself. The corporation is at an end, both its soul and body cease as a whole, but the immortal constituents do not cease and never will. . . . Our mistake has been in not seeing that death is indeed, like birth, a salient feature in the history of the individual, but one which wants exploding as the end of the individual, no less than birth wanted exploding as his beginning."

Belief in Reincarnation should save us from the fear of death, and from undue grieving for loved ones who have died. The Chinese philosopher Chuang Tzu was censured by a friend because, so far from mourning for his wife, he celebrated her death by singing and drumming on an inverted bowl.

"You misjudge me," said Chuang Tzu. "When she died, I was in despair, as any man well might be. But soon, pondering on what had happened, I told myself that in death no strange new fate befalls us. In the beginning we lack not life only, but form. Nor form only, but spirit. We are blent in the one great featureless, indistinguishable mass. Then a time came when the mass evolved spirit, spirit evolved form, form evolved life. And now life in its turn has evolved death. For not nature only but man's being has its seasons, its sequence of spring and autumn, summer and winter. If someone is tired and has gone to lie down, we do not pursue him with shouting and bawling. She whom I have lost has laid down to sleep for a while in the Great Inner Room. To break in upon her rest with the noise of lamentation would but show that I knew nothing of nature's Sovereign Law."[1]

I believe that on the astral plane everything that we know on earth has its counterpart. We

---

[1] *The Way and its Power*, p. 54.

meet our friends and our enemies, both those who are alive and those who are dead, and have the power to do good or ill, and so adjust karma or incur new debts.

There are boundless opportunities of helping others away from earth, comforting those in sorrow, giving fresh courage to the faint of heart and the disillusioned, helping to solve the troubles of the perplexed, tending those in suffering. This help may be given both by those who have left their earth bodies in their beds, and by those who are waiting for new bodies in which to incarnate. Everyone knows how a problem which was perplexing him when he fell asleep is sometimes found to be solved when he awakes in the morning. Is it difficult to believe that he has received help away from earth? Thus "gentle sleep, Nature's soft nurse," not only restores the physical body, but "knits up the ravelled sleeve of care" by giving the astral body opportunities of mental and spiritual refreshment.

"If any of you lack wisdom, let him ask of God . . . and it shall be given him." (*James, i,* 5).

But to obtain help of any kind away from earth it is necessary to ask, and to ask with the intensity of a man pleading his cause; mere lip service or vain repetitions will not suffice, but "all things, whatsoever ye ask in prayer, believing, ye shall receive." (*Matthew, xxi,* 22).

Prayer, or calling, as it used to be termed, has been likened to a boat: the person who uses it must furnish it with the oars and compass. Prayer should be explicit and sincere; it should be made with the proviso that the end immediately desired may be ultimately right for him who asks, and he should not be discouraged because it is not immediately granted; but a prayer should not be made at all until the person making it can feel that he has done his best to bring about the desired result by his own efforts. Clearly those away from earth are not to be treated as trouble-savers, nor are they to be expected to gratify a whim, or to help in a task which the applicant might easily perform himself if he took the trouble.

But when the call is earnestly and sincerely sent, then, if the caller's karma entitles him to relief, the prayer will be granted, whether it be made to Jesus, or to another of the Great Masters, or to one whom the caller has known in life upon this earth. To whom it is made does not greatly matter, for it will be received and—if the time is ripe—a helper will be sent: "Behold, the Lord's hand is not shortened, that it cannot save; neither his ear heavy, that it cannot hear." (*Isaiah*, *lix*, 1).

There are millions of these helpers away from earth, ready to respond to calls to aid. They are the angels of the Bible, or messengers, which is the correct translation of the Greek word *angelos*, whence "angel" is derived. "He shall give his angels charge over thee, to keep thee in all thy ways. They shall bear thee up in their hands, lest thou dash thy foot against a stone." (*Psalms*, *xci*, 11–12). Such messengers are not necessarily people who are out of incarnation, since it is possible for everyone to act as a helper while his earth body is asleep, and to aid others in ways which would be impossible on the physical plane.

It may be asked why, if this is so, people do not remember their activities when they are away from their bodies. Some do, just as some remember their past lives. We all dream, but some of us can remember our dreams more accurately than others. This is purely a matter of training. In Ancient Egypt a person who had been trained to remember what he had been doing while away from his earth body was known as a "traveller." This training has been forgotten, but those who have had it in the past will remember their dreams far more easily than others.

The chief difficulty about dreams is that there are two kinds: resurrected impressions of recent earth happenings, and actual experiences on the astral. On that plane it is possible to travel so fast, and to accomplish so much, that it is only with great difficulty that experiences can be checked. It is like travelling in an express train and trying to take in all the scenery at once. The result is that one comes back to one's body with a jumble of recollected experiences, which appear to make nonsense. The only method of remembering these experiences accurately is to write every dream down at the moment of waking, whether it

makes sense or not. If this is done persistently—
and it needs a great deal of determination, which
in itself is excellent discipline—recollection gradually clarifies and the real is sorted from the
unreal.

In this way it is possible to prove that astral experiences are true: for if you dream that you have
been with a friend, helping, let us say, a puzzled
child to work out a sum which he left unfinished
when he went to bed, or doing what you can for
victims of an air bombardment in China (for
those sufferers would be prone to continue their
condition on the astral plane), and if your friend
remembers having had exactly the same dream,
then I consider that this is adequate proof of astral experience: but to make it conclusive each
should have written the dream down separately
and compared it afterwards.

Another test is to ask your friend a question to
which he cannot know the answer. Then tell him
to keep the question in his mind just before he
goes to sleep and to concentrate on a desire to
meet you away from earth, when you promise to

give him the answer. If he does meet you, and remembers the answer on awaking, he must write it
down immediately. If the answer is the correct
one, it must follow, even though you yourself may
not remember answering the question, that your
friend and you did meet away from earth. This,
again, needs patience and training: but it can be
done.

Those who can accept this astral life away from
the physical body will find intense comfort and
happiness in the knowledge that they are able to
meet loved ones who have died, and to help their
fellows away from earth, even though they do
not remember having done so on their return.
Whether they remember or not, is unimportant:
what really matters is that help is given and service rendered; and this, I am very sure, is possible
if the genuine desire be there and is expressed in
thought when one is on the point of falling asleep.
Those who wish to come to fruition quickly will
do so best by asking how they can help others,
both on earth and away from it. On earth opportunities may not readily present themselves,

although seldom can a day go by without a chance of each one of us being able to render some act of kindness to another; but away from earth these opportunities are far greater, and everyone, however weak and humble on earth, has the power to do much.

Never before was the need of such helpers so great as it is to-day; never before, I firmly believe, have there been so many helpers away from earth. Only by helping others can we ascend ourselves. And although, as Krishna and Jesus taught, service must be unselfseeking, nevertheless every act, however small, is noted and will be placed to the credit of the doer when his karma is assessed.

Just as no good action is ever forgotten, so is no lesson ever quite lost, although it may take long to learn it thoroughly; and everything is profitable which demands some kind of effort: it is the effort which counts, rather than the successful result, and success is but the result of many failures.

It is here that Reincarnation holds out the promise of ultimate fulfilment. To some the prospect of having to live through a succession of existences, with their accompanying ills and sufferings, is an appalling thought: but Reincarnation offers compensations which would be impossible if we lived but once: all we have missed, all we have longed to be, to do, to see, to learn in one life, we may be, and do, and see, and learn in lives to come; present frustration means future achievement, failure nothing but the prelude of success. As the poet "A.E." once said, "The romance of your spirit is the most marvellous of stories. Your wanderings have been greater than those of Ulysses."

Before we can hope to reach the end of the journey it is necessary for each of us to know himself—that is to say, to be able to define truthfully the reason for each and every action. That is why it is so necessary—and so difficult—to be honest with ourselves, for most of us incline to self-deception.

Thus we may learn to choose rightly in all circumstances, and thereby learn to control the will, which is the weapon of the spirit. Opportunities are given us every day of learning to be masters of our own will, rather than its slaves: and when we have learned to keep our tempers in the petty irritations of daily life we have gone far towards it. For some this lesson is easier to learn than for others. Some people seem to be born imperturbable. Often they are not the most highly educated, or those we should consider the most intelligent. I remember a Wiltshire sergeant of mine returning from a raid on the Bulgar trenches in Macedonia during the last war. He was carrying a very hot Lewis gun in his arms, and a heavy bombardment was coming from the enemy gunners who had been woken up by the raid and were providing retaliation for their front line trenches. The sergeant remained unmoved.

"They can't get we egzited, zur," he said.

Such imperturbability is as typical of many people who have incarnated in England and Scotland as it is untypical of those in Wales or Ireland, or the Latin countries. The excitable are apt to regard the others as bovine. There is of course a difference between the insensitive person who has no nerves, and the sensitive person who has learned, with effort, to control his nerves and his temper. But it may be that those others have made their effort in the past. As Shelley said,

Man who man would be
Must rule the empire of himself! In it
Must be supreme.

Without such control, mental balance is impossible, and balance is the quality of which to-day we seem to have most need. The astral body runs riot and masters the mental, and so emotion controls thought, instead of thought being controlled by the will. Balance can be achieved by realizing the cause of non-balance. Once it has been attained, clear perception follows, and with it come tolerance, patience and forbearance, ability to understand the faults of others, and so to pardon them, and wisdom to correct our own. With that understanding comes stability: what was once called the ability to stand alone on all planes: the symbol of such a one was the Upright Diamond, a symbol which may be found among the great stones of Avebury to this day.

Understanding and stability gave peace, which is "the contemplation of all tasks successfully accomplished."

"Mark the perfect man, and behold the upright: for the end of that man is peace." (*Psalm, xxxvii*, 37).

To attain this end, incarnation after incarnation is necessary, although how many depends upon the quickness with which the lessons are learned. As to the intervals between incarnations, there have been many speculations. The Tibetans believe that the Dalai Lama reincarnates in the body of a new-born child at the moment of death. Others have believed in varying periods, and it seems likely that they are often determined by circumstances, but speaking generally, I believe it to be a period between 150 and 200 years.

When the last incarnation is over, then "shall

the dust return to earth as it was: and the spirit shall return unto God who gave it." (*Ecclesiastes, xii*, 7).

And what, it may be asked, is the end of this achievement? If we accept the fact that we are here to benefit by every experience, and have to come to earth life after life until we have done so, what, then, is the end of it all—all this striving, and care, and bitter suffering and pain that we must endure before we come to fruition? Is so much stress worth what we expect to gain? That, perhaps, is not for us to say. The limitations of human understanding cannot be expected to penetrate the ultimate intentions of God, who is "all we cannot conceive." Perhaps we need not "in all things ask the how and the why and the wherefore." Enough that we try to give a good account of ourselves while we are here and do what we are called upon to do, to the best of our ability. But we may be sure of this: that the ultimate aim, the Nirvana of the Buddhist, the Kingdom of Heaven of the Christian, is not oblivion.

Edward Carpenter pictures attainment thus:

Centuries long in her antechambers tarrying,
Lost in strange mazes, wandering, dissatisfied—
in sin and sorrow, lonely, despised and
fallen—
At length the soul returns to Paradise. . . .
Through the great gates, redeemed, liberated,
suddenly in joy over the whole universe
expanding—after her many thousand years
long exile,
At length the soul returns to Paradise.

I have heard the process of spiritual evolution described as the emergence from a sea of unexpanded consciousness to a sea of expanded and perfected consciousness: a state of being implying completed experience, which, having been gathered, frees man from the necessity of rebirth and affords him peace in omniscience. Each perfected spirit carries with it all the experience gathered in every incarnation, and thus, with millions of other spirits of like experience, forms a mighty force of perfected will, each blending with the whole, yet at the same time retaining its own individuality, like a grain of sand which becomes one with the immensity of the desert, while remaining a grain of sand: what tremendous purpose might not such a mass of perfected will, working in unity, achieve?

"All the rivers run into the sea; yet the sea is not full," said the Preacher. "Unto the place from whence the rivers came, thither they return again."

Acknowledgments

In Chapters Five and Six, the quotations from Sir Edwin Arnold's *Song Celestial* and *Light of Asia* are taken from the editions published by Messrs Kegan Paul, Trench, Trubner and Co., Ltd.

In Chapter Six, I have also quoted from Lafcadio Hearn's *Gleanings in Buddha Fields* (Kegan Paul), *Some Sayings of the Buddha*, translated by F. L. Woodward, M.A. (Oxford University Press), and *Buddha and the Gospel of Buddhism*, by Dr Ananda Coomaraswamy (Harrap). I have also referred to Mr

Acknowledgments

Edward Thompson's delightful book, *The Youngest Disciple* (Faber and Faber).

In Chapter Seven, I have used Dr Lionel Giles's *The Sayings of Lao Tzu* ("Wisdom of the East" series, John Murray), Mr Arthur Waley's *The Way and its Power* (Allen and Unwin), and *Confucius and his Quest*, by Maurice Magré (Thornton Butterworth).

Miss Eva Martin's anthology *The Ring of Return* (Philip Allan) was of great service to me in writing Chapter Nine, and is to be recommended to those in search of further quotations on the subject. I must also make the following acknowledgments for kind permission to use material quoted in this chapter: to Mr Algernon Blackwood and to Messrs Jonathan Cape for the passage from *Episodes before Thirty*; to Messrs George Allen and Unwin for the passage from Edward Carpenter's *Art of Creation*; to Messrs Macmillan for the quotation from "A.E.'s" "In Babylon"; to Mr W. H. Davies and Messrs Jonathan Cape for the quotation from *Later Days*, and finally to Mr John Masefield for permission to quote the two verses from "A Creed" (from *Collected Poems*, Wm. Heinemann, Ltd.).

For general sources I may mention the following:

Acknowledgments

The Human Situation, by Professor W. MacNeile Dixon (Allen and Unwin), *Life After Life*, by Eustace Miles (Norwich Publishing Co.), and *Reincarnation for Everyman*, by Shaw Desmond (Andrew Dakers). Mr Shaw Desmond's book *After Sudden Death* (Andrew Dakers) deals specifically with the difficulties of those who die suddenly and unprepared.

I must express my gratitude for the assistance and encouragement given me by Miss Averil Mackenzie-Grieve while my work was in progress. My thanks are also due to Captain Arnold Kaufman and Miss Dorothea Braby for reading my manuscript and giving me helpful suggestions, and to Mr Arthur Wyeth and Mr Walter Neale, without the guidance of whose wisdom and experience it would not have been possible for me to write this book.

O.R.

THIS EXCLUSIVE EDITION
*has been typeset for The Reincarnation Library
in Berthold Bodoni Antiqua, Bodoni, and
Yorkshire and printed by offset lithog-
raphy on archival quality paper
at Thomson-Shore, Inc.*

*The text and end-papers are acid-free and meet
or surpass all guidelines established by
the Council of Library Resources
and the American National
Standards Institute™.*

Book design by Charlotte Staub